# your
# SIX-YEAR-OLD

# your SIX-YEAR-OLD
## Defiant but Loving

by Louise Bates Ames
and Frances L. Ilg

*Gesell Institute of Child Development*

**Illustrated with photographs
by Betty David**

DELACORTE PRESS/NEW YORK

*To our daughters,*
Joan and Tordis,

*and our grandchildren,*
Carol, Clifford, Douglas, Karl, Mark,
Tommy, and Whittier

Published by
Delacorte Press
1 Dag Hammarskjold Plaza
New York, New York 10017

Manufactured in the United States of America

First printing

*Designed by Giorgetta Bell McRee*

LIBRARY OF CONGRESS CATALOGING IN PUBLICATION DATA

Ames, Louise Bates.
Your six-year-old.

Bibliography: p.
Includes index.
1. Child development. I. Ilg, Frances
Lillian, 1902–    ,joint author. II. Gesell
Institute of Child Development, New Haven.
III. Title.
HQ772.A476        155.4'24        78–11578

ISBN 0–440–09877–7

# CONTENTS

# FOREWORD

Norms, or descriptions, of what a parent may expect his or her child to do at any given age make some people feel secure. They make other people anxious or even angry. But we have found that most parents do seem to find it comforting to know more or less what they may expect of their child at any given age.

Many find it especially comforting when their child is going through a difficult or demanding stage to learn that it is all very "normal"—that other children behave in these ways too.

We ourselves have been studying child behavior for the past forty years or more and our own studies were preceded by those of Dr. Arnold Gesell, the Director of our former Clinic at Yale, in whose honor our present Institute was founded.

All these studies, which have involved literally thousands of boys and girls, have convinced us that human behavior develops in a highly patterned way. It seems quite possible to describe rather clearly the more or less predictable stages through which any kind of behavior— motor, language, adaptive, personal-social—develops.

We can tell you with high confidence what the stages of development will be in the more or less *average* boy or girl.

But of course hardly anybody is truly "average." As we

shall describe in rather great detail in Chapter Nine of this book, *every child is an individual, different in many ways from every other child living—even from his or her own identical twin.*

So when we tell you that Four is wild and wonderful, Five is calm and serene, Six something else again, this does not mean that *all* children at any one of these ages will behave or should behave just exactly in the ways we describe.

Some perfectly normal boys and girls will be ahead of our schedule. Some will be behind, and it is certainly not a cause for concern in either case. And then, of course, there are those who will hit it right on the nose.

Not only will there be many differences in timing, but also in level of equilibrium or disequilibrium. Some children at all ages are charmingly well adjusted, easy to live with. Others, no matter how skillful and caring their parents, may be difficult at any stage of childhood, or at all.

Some children seem to develop in a fairly integrated way. All the different kinds of behavior occur rather evenly. So, they will be right at, or above their age, or below their age in motor, adaptive, language and what we call personal-social behavior. Others may be way ahead of customary expectations in their talking but below age in motor ways. Or just the opposite.

We have described the kinds of individual differences we expect later in this book. But so that no reader will be made anxious by what we say, let us emphasize right here at the very beginning that *the descriptions of expected behaviors which we give are only averages,* generalizations, ways that many of the children we see do conduct themselves.

We have sometimes likened the descriptions we give in this and other similar books to a map of a country through which you may plan to travel. We *can* tell you what the country is like. We *cannot* tell you what your trip will be like. You may go faster or slower than the usual traveler. You may take more side excursions than the average. You may even at times backtrack. The map does not guarantee what you will do or even tell you what you *ought* to do. It merely defines the territory.

Most people find maps quite useful. Many parents find our maps of the terrain of child behavior useful, too. So use our maps if you like and we hope that you will find, as do many, that they provide helpful orientation. Please do *not* use them for comparing your own child with our hypothetical average and then making adverse judgments either about our norms *or* about your own child. Each child is a wonderfully unique and special person. We hope only to help you appreciate him more as he passes through his various stages of development.

# chapter one

# CHARACTERISTICS
# OF THE AGE

Your typical Six-year-old is a paradoxical little person, and *bipolarity* is the name of his game. Whatever he does, he does the opposite just as readily. In fact, sometimes just the choice of some certain object or course of action immediately triggers an overpowering need for its opposite.

The Six-year-old is wonderfully complex and intriguing, but life can be complicated for him at times, and what he needs most in the world is parents who understand him. For Six is not just bigger and better than Five. He is almost entirely different. He is different because he is changing, and changing rapidly. Though many of the changes are for the good—he is, obviously, growing more mature, more independent, more daring, more adventurous—this is not necessarily an easy time for the child.

"Six is a hard age to be," confided one little boy to his mother.

One of the many things that makes life difficult for him is that, as earlier at Two-and-a-half, he seems to live at opposite extremes. The typical Six-year-old is extremely ambivalent. He wants both of any two opposites and sometimes finds it almost impossible to choose.

"I want to and I don't want to," said one little girl when asked at a party why she didn't go to the table and get herself a cookie.

Or, we have a poem by Edna St. Vincent Millay which beautifully characterizes the Six-year-old's difficulty in making a choice:

> "Come along in then, little girl,
> Or else stay out!"
> But in the open door she stands
> And bites her lips and twists her hands
> And stares upon me trouble-eyed:
> "Mother," she says, "I can't decide!
> I can't decide!"

One specific example of Six's oppositeness is his frequent reversal of letters and numbers as he reads or prints. This tendency toward reversal is one of the many reasons why we prefer to delay the formal teaching of reading, both at home and at school. Six's reversals are truly something to be reckoned with.

Six is also stubborn. It is hard for him to make his mind up about big things, but once made up, it is hard to change. About small things, however, he does change rapidly. A choice of vanilla ice cream may immediately lead to a sudden realization that it was really chocolate he wanted all along, and if you change your order to chocolate he may swing back to vanilla.

One of the Six-year-old's biggest problems is his relationship with his mother. It gives him the greatest pleasure and the greatest pain. Most adore their mother, think the world of her, need to be assured and reassured that she loves them. At the same time, whenever things go wrong, they take things out on her.

An example of this is that of the little girl who sat at the dinner table, arms folded, refusing to eat. When her mother urged her to eat, she replied coldly, "How can I? I have no spoon."

At Five, Mother was the center of the child's universe. At Six, things have changed drastically. *The child is now the center of his own universe.* He wants to be first and best.

He wants to win. He wants to have the most of everything.

Six is beginning to separate from his mother. In fact, it is this quite natural move toward more independence and less of the closeness experienced at Five that makes him so aggressive toward her at times. On the other hand, his effort to be free and independent apparently causes him much anxiety. He worries that his mother might be sick or might even die, that she won't be there when he gets home from school. And in his typically opposite-extreme way, one minute he says he loves his mother and the next minute he may say he hates her.

It is not hard to understand why this strong emotional warmth toward and love for his mother, which occurs at the same time he is trying to learn to stand on his own feet, causes him much confusion and unhappiness. It is fair to say that Six is typically embroiled with his mother. He depends on her so much, and yet part of him wishes he didn't.

But Mother is by no means his only problem. The consensus is that somewhere around Five-and-a-half to Six years of age many children's behavior takes a marked turn for the worse in many directions. A list of just a few of the ways in which one very nice little girl changed at this time includes the following:

1. To begin with, and quite uncharacteristically for her, she started crying about almost everything. She cried because she didn't want to go to school (she who had gone with the greatest enthusiasm at Four and Five). She cried about getting dressed. She cried because she couldn't get through breakfast in time to get to school. She cried because school was too hard.
2. For the first time in her life she refused to stay put once she had been put to bed, and often got up and came downstairs—against orders—half a dozen times or more in an evening. Even when she did finally decide to stay in bed, she remained awake, talking endlessly and loudly.

*4*

3. Previously a good eater, she would dawdle and fuss throughout each meal, spoiling the whole meal situation for everybody else at the table.

4. For the first time since she was Two-and-a-half years of age, she would, if left alone in her parents' bedroom, raise havoc among her mother's belongings— especially with dresses and shoes.

5. For the first time ever, she consistently refused to "mind" her mother.

6. Quite unlike herself, she fought and fussed with her playmates, and seemed quite incapable of playing peaceably.

7. To make things even worse, her customary excellent

health gave way to an almost continuous series of earaches and sore throats.

*(And every single one of these difficulties cleared up by the time she was Seven.)*

Things often get so bad around the house that, as one mother put it, "Each morning I get up with the solemn promise to myself to try to make my daughter feel loved. And I may succeed for an hour or so. But then she'll do something so impossible that I lose my temper and have to reprimand her. Then she accuses me of not loving her. *She* can do anything she wants, but *my* behavior toward her has to be perfection or she complains."

One of the things that bothers parents most is the child's "freshness." "Why do you want to know?" he or she asks pertly. "Why should I?" "Try and make me." And when things go really wrong, "I love you" changes all too quickly to "I hate you."

But, rather sadly and touchingly, often when the child has been at his worst, once his temper calms down he will ask, "Even though I've been bad, you like me, don't you?" Or, somewhat inappropriately, at the end of a very bad day a child will ask his mother, "Have I been good today?" It is an interesting fact about child behavior that the less praise and credit a child deserves, the more he wants and needs. The very difficult child needs a great deal of assurance that he has been good.

We must remember that a Six-year-old isn't violent, loud, demanding, and often naughty just to be bad. There are so many things he wants to do and be that his choices are not always fortunate. He is so extremely anxious to do well, to be the best, to be first, to be loved and praised, that any failure is very hard for him.

He is, part of the time, demanding and difficult because he is still, even at this relatively mature age, extremely insecure, and his emotional needs are great. If, with tremendous patience and effort, you can meet these needs, nobody can be a better, warmer, more enthusiastic companion than your Six-year-old girl or boy.

Six's way is, in his opinion, right; he cannot bear to lose or to accept criticism. On the other hand, he loves to be flattered and praised. Certainly he is not as secure as he might be. In fact, we believe that much of his stubborn, arrogant, and sometimes bratty behavior is his effort to build himself up and to make himself feel secure. Certainly when he boasts that some certain task imposed on him is "easy," one can suspect that he is trying to cover up the fact that it is actually too difficult.

The typical Six-year-old tends to be highly undifferentiated—everything is everywhere. He seems to have little feeling for scale or hierarchy. He may be displeased because his mother or father has more possessions than he does. (In fact, this attitude may be one thing that leads to his occasional pilfering.)

The child of this age is really a very vulnerable little person, very sensitive emotionally, especially when he is being good. Very small failures, comments, or criticisms hurt his feelings. But if he is being naughty, once he gets started on a bad tack, he may seem almost impervious to punishment. That is why he needs so very much protection and understanding from his parents.

Six, for all he may be so bold and brash at times, tends to be very babyish about physical hurts. He may cry his head off just about having a very small splinter removed from his finger or about having to use nose drops.

However, for all we have said, Six can at times be a delightful addition to the household. One of his most endearing qualities is his extreme enthusiasm. He is enthusiastic for adventure, for new games, for new ideas. He loves to practice and show off his increasing academic abilities. He loves to ask questions. He loves to be read to. He loves to learn about things.

Another of his attractive characteristics is his emotional warmth. When things are right between him and his parents, as of course they often are, nobody could love a

grown-up with more warmth and openly expressed affection. And sometimes he can be a wonderfully warm, loyal, and admiring friend.

He is at his most lovable when he dramatizes something he is telling you: "The biggest one you ever saw!" "The most wonderful time I ever had."

When happy, he not only smiles and laughs, he fairly dances with joy. Even when asleep he seems to pitch his whole body into his dreams—which may explain why his nightmares, when he has them, bother him so much.

His enthusiasm is contagious. Things mean so much to him that it is a pleasure to provide for him opportunities to feed his very real need for the new and the exciting.

Life is seldom dull for the parents of a Six-year-old.

## SIX-AND-A-HALF TO SEVEN

From some of the things we've been saying you might get the impression that we are not really wild about the Six-year-old.

On the contrary! He or she can be one of the nicest, warmest, friendliest, most delightful little persons in the world. Give us a choice of somebody to spend an afternoon with and it might well be Mr. or Miss Six-year-old.

Even on bad days, those warm ways show through, and as Six moves on toward Six-and-a-half he may well shine in all his glory.

Five by nature tends to be quiet and restrained, calm, obedient, *good!* Six can, oh so often, be expansive and out-of-bounds, contrary, violent, hard for a mother to live with. And then by Seven he withdraws once again, and tends to be quiet and subdued.

But somewhere between the perhaps too exuberant and aggressive personality of Six and the often rather melancholy age of Seven comes this delightful time when all the lively, exuberant responses characteristic of this age come to full flower.

In other words, Five was lovable but sometimes a little bland. Early Six was a handful. Six-and-a-half can be truly gorgeous.

What makes him so much fun? His lively intellectuality, for one thing. Intellectual tasks are now a challenge. He *loves* to count for you, loves to say his ABCs, is proud as punch of any reading he can do. He is as proud of his newfound abilities as if he had discovered America.

He is amusing and has a wonderful sense of humor. If you want to be really appreciated, make a joke to a Six-and-a-half-year-old. He will be convulsed with laughter, will tell everybody. You will feel like the most amusing person alive.

Or he loves to play guessing games with you: "What am I thinking of, in this room, which is blue?" "Name some part of me that begins with N." The possibilities are endless, and he enjoys these games so much that you will enjoy them, too.

Five may think you are perfect. Seven won't be quite sure. But the Six-and-a-half-year-old child likes you and you like him. No question. There is a warmth at this age quite unlike anything seen at most other ages.

For a brief little time here the child relates to you, and you are able to relate to him, almost as if he were another, very sympathetic, appreciative, and satisfactory adult. There is a certain maturity to the child of this age that is very appealing.

Though the negative aspect of Six's opposite extremes may have been trying, the positive part is very easy to take: biggest hugs; most "I love you, Mummy"s; worries that something may happen to Mother; boundless enthusiasm for any prospect or proposal; love of exploration, physical and intellectual.

The child of this age loves new places, new ideas, new bits of information, and (his own) new accomplishments. His capacity for enjoyment is tremendous. Make him a present or surprise, give him praise, propose a treat, and his vigorously expressed joy and enthusiasm will well repay you.

Parents, remembering the struggles they sometimes have had with their Six-year-olds, tend to forget the good times. All too many, looking back, remember their Six-year-old as argumentative, oppositional, violent, tantrumy, difficult. And then they think of Seven as silent, withdrawn, suspicious, complaining. They forget, as each

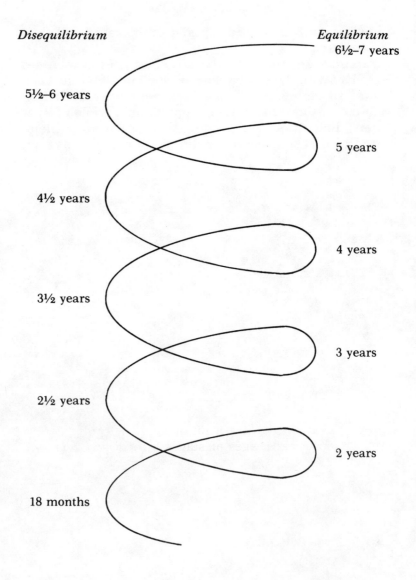

*Disequilibrium*

*Equilibrium*
6½–7 years

5½–6 years

5 years

4½ years

4 years

3½ years

3 years

2½ years

2 years

18 months

*Figure 1*

*Alternation of Ages of Equilibrium and Disequilibrium*

new age brings its demands on parental forbearance and fortitude, that there was, for many, this brief, blissful, enthusiastic, warmly responsive, and exciting time when son or daughter was Six-and-a-half.

Glimpses of perfection in the parent-child relationship tend to be brief. But Six-and-a-half can be, if you're lucky, one of the nicest and most rewarding periods in early childhood.

WARNING!

Here, as for every age we describe in any of our books, we must give an important warning. *Do not take too seriously what anybody (we included) tells you about how your child will or may behave.*

Child behavior, for all reasonably normal children, does develop in a patterned way. Stages of equilibrium are followed by stages of disequilibrium which must occur before the child can reach some succeeding stage of equilibrium. (See Figure i.) That this will happen we are reasonably sure. And we can tell you approximately when these things will happen in the usual course of development.

What we cannot tell you is exactly when they will occur in your own individual child. Nor can we tell the extent to which either breakup or adjustment will go. Some children seem always to live a bit on the side of disequilibrium. Even at calm ages or stages they do have trouble with themselves and those around them.

Other children, even in the same family, may always seem to live on the brighter side of life. Living is easy for them; people and things do what they expect. It is easy for them to be good.

We tell you about behaviors characteristic of the different ages not so that you will check and worry. We tell you what behavior is usually like so that you can, within reason, know what to expect and then *not* worry when your own child's behavior, as it is bound to now and then, departs from the ideal.

# chapter two

## THE CHILD AND OTHER PEOPLE

Your Six-year-old, in his typically opposite-extreme way, is at his best and at his worst with other people. Nobody is a more lively, enthusiastic, enjoyable, and rewarding son or daughter; nobody a nicer student; nobody a warmer friend. And yet at times any or all of these relationships can go bad at the same time, putting a great strain on those around him.

First of all, consider Six and his mother, already discussed in some detail in the preceding chapter. Of all the interpersonal relationships the young child experiences through the first ten years of life, that between his mother and himself is probably the most important and intense.

Six is one of the ages when child and mother are most closely involved. He wants to be close to her and yet at the same time he wants his independence. So, as we have pointed out, at Five, Mother is the center of the young child's world. At Six, he is the center of his own world.

This involves some breaking away, some tug and pull. The child of Six finds his center, stability, equilibrium, focus, and status in his relationship with his mother. And yet, as growth propels him to increasing maturity and independence, he feels impelled to break away and establish his own independence.

So we have the conflicts and ambivalence which characterize mother-child relationships at Six. The child loves his mother and needs her. He *must* be assured of her love and acceptance. But at the same time, in his drive for self-dependence, he often behaves toward her in a way that makes life hard for Mother and for himself.

*Father* is also a much-loved person at this age, and his time and attention are much sought after and highly prized by both girls and boys. In fact, some are too demanding and want more of his time than he can comfortably give. Many fear their father's disapproval more than that of their mother, and admire him more than they do her. Many children think their father knows everything—even what goes on at home while he is at work.

However, some fathers find their Six-year-olds hard to get along with. They may, for instance, find his (or her) intense desire to be noticed especially trying. They may also be particularly disturbed by the fact that many Sixes are poor sports (cannot stand to lose in a competitive situation), are not always honest (they frequently steal small sums of money or trinkets from parents' desks or bureaus), and do not always tell the truth.

Mothers, if they are at home with the child most of the day, are more ready to accept the customary immaturity expressed in these ways. Fathers are more likely to come in with a strong "It's time that he (she) did so-and-so."

In other words, fathers in general, unless they are very easygoing, are often less patient than mothers with the difficult side of this age. Sixes, being rather sensitive about what they can and cannot get away with, may behave better with Father than with Mother, at least much of the time.

So there is often a startling improvement in the smoothness and ease of bath or bedtime when Father takes over on occasion. It is important to keep in mind, however, that if he should take over on a regular basis, the likelihood is that all the tug and pull of the child's daily relationship with Mother would then be transferred to him. It seems to be the main caretaker who gets the worst of it with the child of this age.

This is one reason why Aunt or Grandmother who may, in Mother's absence, be able to manage some bit of the daily routine with little difficulty, should not feel too superior about her success. Six is at his best and also his worst with the *primary* caretaker.

It can be very useful to keep in mind that when the going gets tough, it can work best to have the child spend some time with just one parent. And since most at Six are not as embroiled with Father as they are with Mother, and also tend to be a bit more in awe of him, if a tantrum or big problem threatens, Father may be the one who saves the day.

GRANDPARENTS

A Six-year-old, with all his warmth and love and emotion, can be extremely appreciative of Grandmother or Grandfather. If either tries too hard to boss, a child may respond with snippy remarks. But on the whole the relationship is smooth and heartwarming.

Most Sixes love to visit their grandparents or love to have their grandparents visit them. One such child, when his sister said she wished Grandma lived nearer so they could see her every day, replied, "That would spoil it all. Then we would just be running in there all the time and take her for granted and she wouldn't seem so special."

Another Six-year-old girl, when her grandmother was visiting, said to her brother, "What wonderful person do you think is coming down the stairs? Oh, it's just Daddy."

For all the warmth that very often does exist between grandparent and child, when questioned about grandparents, children tend to say, as at Five, that the best thing they like about their grandmother is that she "makes us good food and gives us things." About Grandpa they say, "He gives us things."

They say they like to visit grandparents because of the

good food and getting to play with their cousins. Descriptions of grandparents are still at a physical level, mostly in terms of the color of hair or eyes. So: "She has short blond hair, wears shoes, wears dresses"; "Has curly hair with just a little white"; "She wears glasses—is old—makes good food"; "Nice to me; buys me ice cream." A few go so far as to say, "He's very handsome, very nice," or "She's beautiful."

A special suggestion to grandparents—when possible, restrict visits of grandchildren to one at a time. A single grandchild acts entirely differently alone with his grandparents. The presence of a sibling may simply extend their normal quarreling to the grandparents' home.

### TEACHER

Paradoxically, that Six-year-old who may be such a terror (at times) at home may be a perfect little lady or gentleman at school. We often notice this phenomenon—that a marked change in behavior related to age occurs first at home and only later at school. (We see it later on when the breakup at Eleven or the withdrawal so characteristic of Thirteen occurs at home, often quite a few months before one sees it at school.)

Most Sixes want to be "good" in school and to do what their teacher tells them to. They want to conform, and may even feel rather secure if the teacher is especially strict.

In school, as elsewhere, they want to do well, to be praised and complimented.

One problem that sometimes arises is that to many at this age the teacher's word is law, her way of doing things the "right" way. So, if as is sometimes the case, the rules which predominate at home are different from those at school, the child may get confused about which ones to go by. When Mother's way and Teacher's way differ, it is up to the mother and/or teacher to try to straighten things out for the child. It is unfair to expect a child of Six to make the discrimination that you behave one way at home and quite another way at school.

Show and tell is very important, and it is especially important to Six that his teacher as well as classmates show an interest in whatever it is he may have to share.

Though, as noted, his teacher's word is law and he usually likes and respects her, the relationship of the first-grader to his teacher may not be as intense and personal as it will be in another year.

And, even when all-day first grade overtires the child, as it often does, he seldom takes his fatigue and frustration

out on the teacher. Instead, he waits till he gets home and then "takes it out" on Mother.

SIBLINGS

Though sometimes things go well, the typical Six-year-old is not at his best with siblings, especially with younger siblings. He may show a certain respect for those older, and at times may be very kind to younger ones. For instance, he may enjoy teaching them things.

But on the whole, his competitive, combative nature, and his need always to be first and to win out, make certain difficulty in the household. Sometimes his whole day may

be spoiled if a sibling gets to the table before he does, or receives a bigger piece of cake. He tends to be very jealous of attention or objects given to a brother or sister. It may make him very angry if a sibling is allowed to make a visit or go on an outing from which he himself is excluded.

Six may be very bossy with younger siblings. He may argue, tease, bully, frighten, torment, get angry, hit.

FRIENDS

Other children mean a lot to Six-year-olds, but again the very nature of Six makes it hard for him to get on well with others. Two children together may make out very well, at least for a time, but three tend to make trouble.

"Are you playing with So-and-so?" is a constant refrain. (The idea being, as it will be again at Eleven, that if you are playing with So-and-So you can't play with me.)

Friends mean a lot to the child of this age, and some make friends (even though they can't always keep them) quite easily. As one little girl explained to her mother, "It's very easy to make friends. You just go up to somebody and say, 'Will you be my playmate?' and they say 'Yes.' " Some, in fact, think so much of their friends that they may fall under the spell of some one (often, from the parents' point of view, unsuitable) friend.

But much of any playtime tends to be rather stormy. Children of this age tend to be very aggressive both verbally and physically. They are also quarrelsome, belligerent, boisterous, argumentative, excitable, emotional. Since Six always wants to win, any kind of competitive game may give trouble, and the loser tends to go away mad. Six wants to boss and to win. This does not make him an easy friend to get along with. It is not enough for him to win two games out of three; he wants to win all three. In order to be sure to win, he is not above cheating. This does not make for easy relationships. Six-year-old play quite characteristically rings with cries of "You're cheating. I won't play with you." Some Sixes solve their problem by making up their own rules.

Six-year-olds usually have little sense of humor with friends and little ability to forgive. "I shouldn't have scolded Francine for tearing my paper dolls," says Six-year-old Abbie to her mother. "Why not, dear?" asks Mother, hoping that at last Abbie is becoming more tolerant of her friend's behavior. "Because I think it was really Nancy who tore them," replies Abbie.

Children of this age are excessively interested in and critical of the conduct of friends: "Look at her; she thinks she's everything." Or even, "She thinks she's a princess with those curls of hers bobbing up and down but she isn't. You ought to see her drawing." A child whom adults often consider more than a little "fresh" herself is apt to accuse her friends of being fresh.

Also, though sometimes kind and helpful with younger children, most are extremely aware of the importance of being Six, like the boy who had his birthday a week before his friend. He commented to his mother, of that friend, "A Five-year-old should know better than to argue with me."

The Six-year-old is all too often rough in play. He threatens to go home, quarrels, calls names, pushes, fights. He definitely complains, as noted, that others are cheating and don't follow the rules. And some are very mean to younger children. Fortunately, both grudges and memories tend to be short, and friendships are often resumed on a day following tremendous complaint and conflict.

There is definitely some grouping by sexes in play; that is, girls probably play most with other girls, boys with other boys, though much play crosses sex lines. A few girls have boyfriends and there is some talk of marriage—though marriage talk quite as often involves doll or paper-doll play as it does other real children.

For all the conflict that may occur, it can truly be said of the typical Six-year-old that he has trouble living with his friends, but that he definitely can't live without them.

# chapter three

# ROUTINES, HEALTH, AND TENSIONAL OUTLETS

EATING

Your Six-year-old at the table is something else again. And we might as well discuss his table manners because these are what bugs most parents the most. Knowing about what to expect won't necessarily change the behavior, but it may make you less angry about it.

Don't be surprised when your Six-year-old stuffs his mouth, talks with his mouth full, grabs for food, knocks over his milk, dribbles, kicks the chair leg, teeters back in his chair, and, all too often, even falls off his chair.

"Why, what are you doing down on the floor?" asked one very patient father of a Six-year-old. His daughter couldn't exactly explain, but she looked a little embarrassed and mightily relieved that her father didn't scold her.

In addition to his other misdemeanors he tends to eat very slowly. And he often fights with his siblings if there are any around. Also he tends to refuse to use his napkin, which he actually needs very much.

All of his actions do not bother *him* too much, but he does mind all the scolding, and the more he gets scolded, the more uncoordinated his behavior tends to become.

However, we can say for the Six-year-old that he tends to be a "wonderful" eater, if we are thinking about amount

of food consumed. Many Six-year-olds love to eat and may seem to be eating all day long. Admittedly, their eyes may be bigger than their stomachs, so they often help themselves to more food than they can actually eat. And, grabby as he often is, Six wants the biggest piece. If there are other siblings near his age, some quarreling may go on about the size of portions, especially of desserts.

Though Six may have a rather wide range of things he likes in the way of food and may sometimes be willing to try new things, likes and dislikes are for the most part rather definite. So most Sixes like meat, potatoes, milk, raw vegetables, peanut butter, ice cream, candy and usually hate cooked desserts and cooked vegetables. As when he was younger, the child specially dislikes lumpy and stringy foods, or may refuse meat because once he was given a piece of meat with a little fat on it.

Self-help is not as good as many parents hope. Certainly Six cannot yet cut his meat, and sometimes he may even regress to the point of giving up his spoon or fork and eating with his fingers. Some even eat mashed potatoes with their fingers. A fork may be used willingly if food is of a kind which can be speared.

SLEEPING

Though most Five-year-olds go to bed without much trouble, along about Five-and-a-half some problems may arise. It isn't so much that they resist going to bed—in fact, their customary late-day fatigue may make the idea quite welcome. But some become surprisingly fearful around this age, and need the company of their mother even after the lights are turned off. Often a night-light, or a familiar stuffed animal or doll, helps them a lot.

By Six, bedtime may become one of the nicest times of the day. The child, as a rule, goes to bed quite willingly and without the delaying tactics so conspicuous during the preschool years.

Some like to take a book to bed with them, but many

prefer having a good long chat with Mother. Six likes to show you how well he can count. In fact, he may especially enjoy having Father put him to bed so they can do arithmetic together. He also likes to demonstrate his beginning reading abilities.

But even more than that, if the day has been tangled, as it often has, he likes to use this occasion as a making-up time with Mother. Even a most unhappy day can be rounded off happily by a nice conversation with her.

Very, very few Sixes now have an afternoon nap, so most are well ready for bed by seven or eight o'clock.

Many at Six are said not only to be "wonderful" eaters but "wonderful" sleepers as well. Many sleep nicely right through the night. Not as many seem to have disturbing bad dreams and nightmares as was the case just earlier, but most, if they do, can be calmed by parents. Some are very easily calmed; others like to get into their parents' bed. If the child has a good history of being willing to sleep in his or her own bed, it is usually fine to permit this. It seldom becomes a habit.

Children vary in sleep needs, but eleven hours is an average amount of night sleep. Morning waking time varies somewhat, but most, when they do wake, can take care of themselves and do not bother parents. Most are more interested in reading or playing than in dressing themselves, but if clothes are laid out for them, some will dress themselves without too much fuss.

ELIMINATION

Either day or night wetting is rather rare. A child may delay too long, because he is so busy, and then may have to make a mad dash for the bathroom. Some may need to be reminded by parents to go to the bathroom before they go out to play or for a long trip.

A daytime accident, especially under tension at school, is not unusual. When this happens, the child is much ashamed and must be made to feel that it is perfectly okay and not an uncommon occurrence.

Many now sleep right through the night without getting up for toileting. Those who do need to get up may be able to take care of their own needs, but if the bathroom is not too handy, may still need help.

It is not unusual for even a Six-year-old to be still wetting the bed. If parents cannot wait any longer for all-night dryness, some may like to purchase and try one of the good conditioning devices which have helped so many.* However, we ourselves prefer to give the child one more year to make dryness on his own, and so prefer to wait till Seven to try one of these devices.

In general, bowel control gives little difficulty. Many children function at or around some certain time of day, but this varies from child to child. Little help is needed in this department except for the fact that some children do have accidents, especially at or on the way home from school. This causes even more embarrassment and concern than mere pants wetting.

When it does occur, parents can help by trying to see that their child has a bowel movement at home before he or she goes to school. Some children have trouble managing this on the school toilet, and these children often get into difficulty on the way home from school, especially if they take a roundabout route or play along the way.

Any accident such as this should not be met with scolding. Rather, parents should attempt to plan things better so that it will not be repeated. Interestingly enough, swearing and name calling are often related to the bowel function at this age. "Stinker" is a term in common use and

---

*The two devices which we most frequently recommend are U-Trol, distributed by J. G. Shuman Associates, Box 306, Scotch Plains, New Jersey 07076, and Dry-O-Matic, distributed by Dry-O-Matic Company, 610 Allcott, Marshall, Michigan 49068. Either can be bought for under fifty dollars.

may well stem from something that has actually happened.

Most children will, if reminded, even though perhaps a bit reluctantly, wash up before mealtimes. But the nightly bath, which earlier may have been much enjoyed, may now be resisted. In fact, it may be resisted to the point that some mothers find it easier to give a bath every other night instead of nightly.

Some children show no interest whatever in bathing themselves, whereas others try to take over completely. Others limit their efforts to just some few parts of their bodies. Even the most independent will need help in drawing the bath, and with those finishing touches in the head and neck region.

If Father is willing to take over, often a bath goes more smoothly and quickly with him than with Mother. Though reluctant to take his or her bath, once in the tub the child may dawdle and show no inclination to leave. Things can be speeded up by some such simple technique as counting or planning on an interesting pre-bed activity to follow the bath.

As to dressing, wanting to dress is half the battle—and most could, we assume, if they would. Unfortunately, many have not acquired that desire. Thus there tend to be many battles over dressing. Many need help but may not want to accept it. Sometimes planning that the child will be fully responsible on Tuesday, Thursday, and the weekend and Mother dressing him on Monday, Wednesday, and Friday takes off the strain and works well. The child may be especially expert in dressing over the weekend when he wants to go out to play.

For some, Mother's mere presence is enough—they can do the actual dressing themselves. Many need help with their boots or the second sleeve of their coats.

Girls, especially, tend to get into a real hassle about

*which* dress they are going to wear. Narrowing the choice down to two and then expecting them to change their mind may relieve the tension.

Shoe trouble is very real for both sexes. Boys, especially, like to take their shoes off in the house and then are apt to lose one, or both. Come time for school, a big scramble about "Where did you leave it?" is common.

Though Six is interested in clothes and likes to look well, he or she does not take very good care of them. "She likes to have things right but she doesn't do anything about it," one mother explained it. Thus the typical Six-year-old, in taking clothes off, tends to fling them every which way.

Hair is a problem, but more so with girls than with boys. Boys, for the most part, still wear their hair rather short, so combing or brushing it doesn't take long and is not painful. Those girls who wear long hair fuss and squirm and complain that their mothers are hurting them, as Mother tries to braid or otherwise arrange long hair. The scalp seems to be very sensitive at this time. Sometimes if a girl is given a book to read during the process, it becomes less painful.

TENSIONAL OUTLETS

With all that is going on inside the typical Six-year-old, it is not surprising that tensional outlets, which were at rather a low ebb at Five years of age, but which showed a marked increase at Five-and-a-half, are now at a peak.

Customary tensional outlets at Six range all the way from wriggling and kicking and swinging arms to sharp verbal comments such as "I hate you," to outright temper tantrums. In fact, some Sixes indulge in such horrendously violent tantrums, often striking out at the parent, that Mother may need to take them bodily from the room, leaving them alone for a little so-called time out.

On the other hand if the mother steps in soon enough, before things have become really bad, she can sometimes,

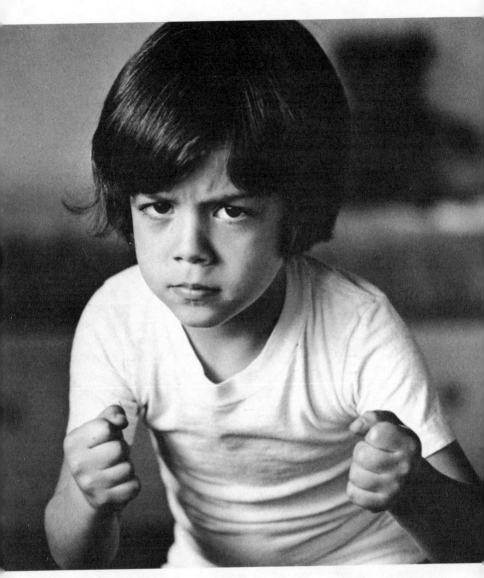

calmly or even humorously, distract the child from whatever it is that so upsets him.

In addition to occasional actual temper tantrums, there are many smaller signs of tension. A child may swing his legs and wriggle, bite or tear at fingernails, scratch, grimace, grind teeth, chew on hair or pencils, pick nose. At the table he may be so restless that he not only kicks the chair leg (or siblings), grabs for and knocks things over on the table, but, as noted, even falls off his chair. (Glasses of milk, especially, should be out of the range of his swinging arms.)

Hands are always busy, especially around the face. Mouth is busy, too. So the child chews fingernails or pencils. Fingernail biting tends to have replaced thumb sucking in most.

Facial grimaces, sometimes almost ticlike in nature, are frequent, and many make numerous, irritating throaty noises or throat clearing. In some there is an increase in, or a return to, stuttering.

To add to all this, many children of this age become suddenly clumsy. In fact, as their mothers put it, they would "fall over a piece of string." Full to bursting of something or other, as many Sixes seem to be, it is perhaps no wonder that we see so much random and unconstructive expenditure of energy. When the child seems most tense, and is engaging in any of these often highly irritating tensional outlets, a parent's kindest course is not to fight against or criticize the outlets, but to try to change the situation as quickly as possible—removing the child to an area of the house or school that will be less overstimulating.

While careful handling will not entirely do away with these tensional outlets, any of them, especially if severe, should be a clue to parent or teacher that the demands of home or school may be too much for the child. He should be protected, within reason, from overdemand.

HEALTH AND SOMATIC COMPLAINTS

With all the other upsets going on at Six, it is probably predictable that health, for many, will take a turn for the worse. It is not just the child's emotions that give trouble, but the very workings of his physical bodily structure.

To begin with, even when not actually ill, he tends to be full of complaints. His legs hurt, his arms hurt, or the back of his neck. And his scalp is very sensitive, especially when hair is being combed.

All mucous membranes seem more sensitive and more easily inflamed than at other ages; eyes may be red and there may be sties. In girls, genitalia become reddened and may need applications of bland salve; nose and throat membranes seem much more sensitive than at other ages. The throat hurts and becomes red and infected, and the infection frequently spreads to ears and lungs. Otitis media (inflammation of the inner ear) again reaches a peak, as it did earlier at Two-and-a-half. And the child complains of being too hot and perspires readily.

Communicable diseases—chicken pox, whooping cough, mumps, diphtheria, and scarlet fever—may all be frequent visitors. Allergy responses are high.

Six not only tires easily, but the very thought of going to school, if the school situation is hard for him, may bring on actual vomiting.

Awkward as he is, there tend to be many falls, cuts, bruises, and scrapes. And he tends to take these badly. The mere sight of blood may be very upsetting to the Six-year-old, and the removal of even a small splinter may bring on a hysterical reaction. Fathers tend to call their sons "sissies" when they overreact to what seems like some rather minor physical damage.

In fact, if you've ever been through the "Mummy likes nose drops! Daddy likes nose drops! Rover likes nose drops!" routine, and your Six-year-old, who has the stuffy nose in the first place, is still resisting their application, you know how hard it is to get medicine into the child of this age. Actually he tends to object to anything which penetrates his body: slivers, enemas, nose drops, what have you. (Similarly he objects to anything which attacks his personality, even the slightest criticism or complaint.)

# chapter four
# TECHNIQUES

There is probably no age at which the use of techniques is more greatly needed or more rewardingly effective. We cannot absolutely *guarantee* their effectiveness, but your chances are excellent that they *will* work.

In fact, it is often little less than miraculous to see a raging tyrant turn into a friendly companion just because you have managed to say or do the right thing.

Technique Number One—*Praise!* It may not be easy to find something you *can* praise, but at least try. We remember one mother whose Six-year-old had been a veritable monster all day long. Come bedtime, he was still carrying on. His mother racked her brain to think of *something* nice she could say about him, and finally hit on it.

"Tommy," she said, "I was very proud of you in school this morning the nice way you said the Lord's prayer." (This was back in the days when children prayed in school.)

Tommy's shouting and tears stopped at once. "Want to hear me say it again?" he asked hopefully. Truly, when things are going very badly, a few words of praise can indeed work wonders.

Next, and another of our favorites, is *Chances.* Many a Six-year-old may meet almost any direct command with "No, I won't." Ignoring this obvious refusal, and refusing to meet resistance head-on, try saying, "I guess you're going to need three chances on that one."

Clearly relieved that he could resist so blatantly, and still have half a chance to avoid open battle, the usual Six-year-old will use up all but his last chance, and then comply with your original request.

*Counting* works almost as well as chances. You ask your boy or girl to do some simple thing. He or she just stands there. So you say, calmly and confidently, "And let's see if you can do it before I count to ten." (Or whatever.)

This gives your child time to pull himself (or herself) together. And allows you to slow down on your counting in case compliance is lagging.

Or, similarly, you can use time marks on the clock: "When the big hand is at the top it will be time to pick up your toys." That is, your child does not have to comply at once, but you have given warning that compliance will eventually be expected.

Technique Number Four is to *Sidestep* the issue. Don't meet violence with violence. Instead of meeting defiance head-on, just change the subject or situation. Many Sixes use up what defiance they have in their initial "No, I won't" or "Try and make me." They may be as relieved as you that war does not have to develop. (Maybe Mother really *is* deaf after all!)

One help to you in sidestepping or dodging the issue is to give as few direct commands as possible. This you will have found useful at earlier ages. And as late as Six, unless a direct command actually needs to be made, you will save time and trouble in giving your orders obliquely.

Technique Number Five is simple—just *Bargain.* You shouldn't depend on this in every situation. It is not only time-consuming but may give the impression of weakness on your part. But at times it works nicely. One little girl we know loved popsicles, and her mother was getting very tired of her asking for them all the time. Finally she bargained: If the little girl would *try very hard* not to fight

with her brother so much, she could have one popsicle every day.

Technique Number Six may indeed seem like weakness to some of you, but it is often highly successful and can provide a wonderfully welcome relief to an embattled mother and child. *Give in.* Sometimes you find yourself giving orders and commands or making rules about things that really don't matter. So if something you have asked

your child to do is greatly resisted, you could pause a moment, think it over and say, "Well, OK, I guess it really doesn't make that much difference."

These are our very best techniques but there are, of course, many other things you can try which are in general use.

*Isolation,* or removing the child from the scene, or just temporarily separating the two of you from each other, can be very effective.

Perhaps one of the most customary techniques used by parents of Six-year-olds is *ignoring.* As at the earlier but similarly difficult age of Two-and-a-half, many parents find that they do best *not to notice* every naughty thing their child does. Some really dangerous behaviors must be checked. But there are other things you really don't like which probably do not actually do major harm. If and when you comfortably can do so, ignore them. Since punishment, though often deserved, does not do much to improve behavior at Six, perhaps the less of it the better.

Experienced parents are usually quite aware of the kinds of situations which bring on their own child's worst behavior. This awareness can help avoid times, places, and arrangements of people which are most certain to arouse disaster.

We give just one example of the kind of situation which is apt to bring on a Six-year-old's worst behavior—loud silly showing off and a total deafness to your commands and suggestions. This may occur whenever company comes. The following are characteristics of the Six-year-old's company behavior:

> He wants to be the life of the party and tends to be irrepressible.
> He likes to bounce his ball in your face, step on your feet, climb all over you, sit on your lap.
> He is likely to interrupt whatever an adult is saying, to monopolize the conversation. Also he likes to show off his gymnastic abilities.

Techniques suggested for guests in the home of a Six-year-old include: (1) Bring him a present. (2) Let him have a turn showing off by bouncing his ball or standing on his head or doing his tricks. (3) Then you—or some other adult —let him take you to his room for a while to show you his toys.

Better to do this early, while he is still on his (relatively) good behavior, than to let things go too far and then have to take him out of the room as a punishment.

And now a few techniques for smoothing out those everyday routines.

*At mealtimes,* when things are so very likely to go wrong because of Six's very active body, relatively poor coordination, and short attention span, the path of wisdom is to have your child sit beside Mother and as far from Father as the size of the table permits. Then Mother can, unobtrusively, give what help is needed, catch that glass before it spills, and give any other assistance required.

It also helps to serve very small portions and then give more if the child wants more, rather than heaping his plate high and then expecting him to finish. Appreciate that some children have very small appetites. And when you can, serve some foods that can be eaten with the fingers.

Ignore poor manners as much as you possibly can. The same amount of effort will pay off much better in another year.

Stomachaches on school mornings can sometimes be prevented or reduced by having the child eat a lighter breakfast. Or by having some admired older child accompany your child to school. A half day only of school helps a lot to reduce the tension which school arouses. And of course it is also important to be sure that your child is not overplaced in school to the extent that school itself is just too much for him.

*Bedtime,* though easy for many, is still a problem for some. It will help, in any event, if Mother can arrange her schedule so that she can spend relaxed time with her child as he reviews his day with her or engages in other enjoyable bedtime chat.

If your boy or girl has trouble getting to sleep or staying asleep, Dr. Lendon Smith, in his excellent book *Improving Your Child's Behavior Chemistry*, recommends that protein nibbling from three o'clock on can help the high-strung child. Old-fashioned peanut butter makes a good snack. Protein for supper, and no dessert or sugar at all, is best. Then at bedtime, a mouthful of cheese or, again, peanut butter or even nuts prevents blood sugar from dropping too low. *If* the child has a good sleep he will not only be more rested in the morning, but more receptive to a good breakfast.

*Dressing.* If your daughter is one of the many with a very sensitive scalp, who screams bloody murder as you comb her hair, a short haircut (if she will accept it) can save much anguish.

If choosing what to wear in the morning is a problem (this occurs with girls more than with boys, as a rule), you can *either* select from the closet just two dresses and tell her she can wear either one she chooses (at least this narrows things down) or, if choices are impossible for her, just firmly pick out the dress she is to wear and tell her that is it.

As mentioned earlier, there will be many *tensional outlets* at this age. When these become extremely violent, you may actually need to pick your child up bodily and take him to his room. If, on the other hand, tensional outlets are relatively mild, it may be best to ignore them as much as possible.

Your very best bet, of course, is to limit the situations which cause the tension in the first place. An occasional day off from school may work wonders. Supper in bed (before the family eats) may bring occasional relief if mealtime with the whole family proves too much of a strain.

*Television,* for all it is so often maligned, can provide an excellent technique for helping your Six-year-old through the day. He can be allowed to watch his favorite program when and if he has completed whatever task you may have in mind for him. Or, if he has been reasonably "good" up till the time his special program begins, he can be allowed to watch it.

But all in all, a mother or father may find that the very best technique is to go a little easy on this poor little fellow who, because of the very immaturities of his age, is often so very hard on himself.

*Ethical Problems.* It must be admitted that Six seems not always able to tell the difference between mine and thine.

In other words, he often steals. Usually this is restricted to taking small sums of money or objects from his parents' bureaus or desks. The best technique in such instances, aside from the usual explanations about not taking things that belong to others, is to lock up desk and bureau drawers. Tell the child you are doing this *to help him remember.*

Most such pilfering is slight and brief. If the child does bring things home from other people's houses you will, of course, see to it that he takes them back, accompanying him if need be.

Another ethical problem quite common at Six is that the child not only does not always tell the truth, but if he does something wrong and you accuse him of it, it is most unlikely that he will admit it. So, if he breaks your favorite vase and you know he did it, don't ask him if he did, because he is almost certain to deny his guilt, even though he may be up to his knees in broken glass. Rather, if you *must* know whether he did it or not, attack the problem in a roundabout way. Ask "How could you reach that vase on that high shelf?" He will, in all likelihood, give some explanation as that he just pushed a chair over to the shelf and climbed up.

# chapter five

## GENERAL INTERESTS AND ABILITIES

Five stayed rather close to home in his accomplishments and abilities. He liked to do the things he was used to and that he knew he could do well. Six is full of adventure and he likes to experiment, likes the new. Almost anything novel will catch and hold his interest—at least until, if it is competitive, somebody beats him at it. Then his composure falters and he may go to pieces. Only to try again tomorrow.

A year ago his play episodes were restricted and confined. They now have scope and movement. His mother says of him, "Whatever he is doing is all over the place."

Six still enjoys many kindergarten-type activities—cutting, pasting, coloring, painting. In fact, he enjoys them with such a passion that he is reported to *love* to color or to paint. Drawings are expansive and imaginative. Boys, especially, like to draw spaceships, airplanes, trains, and boats. Girls still prefer to draw people and houses. (Parents may find that they need a special budget to keep their Six-year-old in supplies for all his activities.)

There is now a return to the preschooler's love of dirt and water. Six-year-olds love to dig in the mud and to make mud roads and houses. Some get so involved with their digging that the holes they make are deeper than their parents prefer. Digging may, in summer, evolve into a little rudimentary gardening, but Six does not always finish what he begins. His eyes are bigger than his stomach, as it were.

The same goes for pets—much wanted, little cared for, though deeply loved.

Six-year-olds are by no means any longer satisfied with their tricycles. If a bicycle has not been provided at Five, there will be much teasing for one at Six. Some are fully ready now for a small bike, but some are not. Some parents find that if the child can have the use of a small, borrowed bicycle, this urge for bicycling can be satisfied, and the actual purchase of a bike of one's own can be put off for another year.

Both boys and girls are full of action at this age. Though both will spend many happy hours indoors at their drawing and painting and other creative activities, both love to be outdoors, tearing around. Sometimes this activity takes the shape of tag or hide-and-seek or roller-skating, swinging, swimming, doing tricks on an outdoor gym. Sometimes it is more formless—activity for the sake of activity itself.

Though both sexes may be interested in ball play, in general it is boys who play ball, girls who jump rope or play hopscotch.

Dress-up play is still a favorite, and now fairly elaborate imaginative games of school are added to the earlier playing house. Girls, especially, enjoy elaborate dress-up play. They particularly favor fancy hats, their mothers' shoes, lipstick.

Doll play is now very big with girls; in fact, for many it is at its height. There is much dressing and undressing of dolls, and nude dolls (which most adults detest) often clutter the playroom or the child's bedroom. Girls are much interested not only in their dolls but in all the things which "belong" to the doll as its clothes, suitcases, furniture—

anything that will enliven the game. Many have begun on paper dolls, though this interest may be much stronger at Seven.

Boys as well as girls enjoy playing house and school, though they may prefer something a bit more active as cowboys, cops and robbers, and war. Shooting the enemy and getting under cover are two favored activities, regardless of what parents may think of this kind of play.

There are so many things that the typical Six-year-old likes to play that it is impractical to try to list them all. Boys like trains; both sexes may enjoy block play or carpentry activities.

Though emotionally not well suited to competitive play, Six, nevertheless, very much enjoys table games with cards, dominoes, or Chinese checkers. Unfortunately, he (or she) cannot *bear* to lose; may cheat in order to win; and if that doesn't work, may dissolve in tears and claim that the other person has cheated. (An understanding and loving grandparent can be the most fun to play with. He or she may be willing, sometimes, to lose.) At any rate, whoever the partner, Six likes to change the rules of the game in order to favor his own chances to win. Puzzles may be safer since they involve less competition.

Wind-up or electric trains are favored by boys, and both sexes enjoy their "collections"—collections which even at Six tend to be rather rudimentary and not well classified.

READING

Books are great favorites with nearly all Six-year-olds. Some may still like to be read to; others may prefer picking out what words and letters they can manage; and some are already quite skilled at reading for themselves, though they like to share and show off this ability to their parents. Some now make good use of the public library, but most love to have their "own" books. Fortunately, nowadays many of the classic children's books are available in paperback form.

Six's reading interests are wide. He still shows interest in the books he liked when only Four or Five but now, especially if reading has been stressed in school and he or she is, by nature, an early reader, some enjoy such books as the *I Can Read* series.

Stories about animals, bugs, and birds are still great favorites, as, for instance, Carle's *The Grouchy Ladybug,* Jewell's *Cheer Up, Pig!,* Kraus's *Kittens for Nothing,* or the always popular Edna Miller *Mousekin* tales.

A little mystery or excitement is also favored, as in Kellogg's *The Mystery of the Missing Red Mittens,* Pinkwater's *Around Fred's Bed,* or Schweninger's *The Hunt for Rabbit's Galoshes.*

In fact, Six's reading tastes are so very catholic that almost any book will be a success with some, provided the words are not too long and the pictures plentiful and dramatic. Six seems ready for almost anything, in reading as in other areas of living.

MUSIC, RADIO, AND TELEVISION

Six, like Five, may like fooling around with the piano, but most are not ready for anything very serious in the way of piano playing. Most still enjoy their own phonograph records.

But the majority prefer either radio, especially if they have their own small radio or, above all, television. TV is an important feature in the lives of most Six-year-olds. Most admit that they watch "a lot," though the actual number of hours spent varies greatly from household to household.

Nearly all have their own preferred programs—"Bugs Bunny," "The Flintstones," the Saturday cartoons. Some are beginning to like the simpler kinds of family-type programs, though most dislike the news and grown-up programs.

Both boys and girls now admit that their parents sometimes object both to the amount of watching they do and

at least to some of the programs they watch. Girls *claim* that they themselves mostly make the final decision as to what they watch. Boys, perhaps more truthful, admit that they and their parents *together* decide what programs can be watched.

Typical of Six's comments about television viewing are
the following. Girls say, "My parents decide how much
watching but I pick my programs out," "Mostly I watch
just weekends," "I don't get to watch what I want to because I have two brothers," "I decide except we have a rule
in our house—whoever gets to the den first, we have to
watch what they choose."

Boys say, "My parents decide everything," "Decide? Half
and half—me and my parents," "Sometimes I don't even
like to watch," "What do I dislike? Whatever my father
changes it to," "I prefer radio because I don't have to wear
my glasses," "It varies who decides—parents, brother, sister, me."

CREATIVITY

"Creativity is an attitude. It springs from the impulse of every human being to communicate in some appropriate form his own absolutely unique experience—unique because there has never been, since the beginning of time, anybody just like him. Every child longs, in effect, to put his thumbprint on the page, to scrawl his message on the world's surface: I WAS HERE."[1]

And nobody fits this description much better than the egocentric, expansive, imaginative Six-year-old who just *must* communicate and create.

We see it in his enthusiastic first-grade drawings—those bright, lively, scenes he draws or paints with sun-enlivened sky, clouds, trees, houses, grass, flowers, each in its separate horizontal row. He (or she) loves to create these scenes and loves to bring them home so that parents can admire them.

How to help your Six-year-old develop and keep alive that creative spirit? First of all, provide materials—water paints, finger paints, crayons, pencils, paper, clay; things to fold, things to cut out and sew, things to pound, and things to model; wires, magnets, magnifying glass, puzzles.

Drawing can be creative, but so can climbing and tumbling on a jungle gym. Many Sixes are quite ready to experiment with the simpler musical instruments. Even playing house and playing school (even playing doctor) can be creative experiences. Sixes love to dress up and pretend they are somebody else, or that simple blocks or boxes and other everyday materials are something other than what they actually are.

Puppets and paper dolls can help the Six-year-old develop his or her strong dramatic interests.

But it is difficult to create in a vacuum. Rich experiences in living are, in most instances, necessary if a child of any age is to develop his or her creative talents to their fullest.

You as a parent don't "teach" your child to create. But

you can, if you wish, provide an atmosphere which helps creativity to develop.

Drawing, painting, singing, playing musical instruments, dancing, and writing are among the kinds of activity which we think of most often when we think of creativity. Some parents who have never considered themselves creative feel at a loss when it comes to helping their children develop this talent.

For such parents it is important to appreciate that creativity, like children themselves, comes in all shapes and sizes. It is reassuring to the mother or father who does not feel like a creative person to realize that creative imagination can be expressed in words as well as in actions.

Milton Young in his excellent *Buttons Are to Push: Developing Your Child's Creativity* gives some good suggestions as to things that any parent can try with a Six-year-old. Here are some of his best:

1. Present your child with a real problem. Try out some of his solutions so that he can learn how to test ideas.
2. Encourage your child to make up a simple code and to use this code to write messages for you or his friends.
3. Ask him to figure out ways he might learn if there were no schools.
4. Work with your child in making models of such things as boats or planes.
5. Discuss the rules of some simple game. Ask your child how the game might be made more interesting by changing the rules.
6. Ask him what he would do in a certain (imaginary) difficult situation, as, for instance, if he ran out of food in a forest or a bear walked into your house.
7. Plan to go on a camping trip. Have children help figure out things you would need.
8. Encourage your child to plan a play. Let him choose the story and characters. Or, have him make up an imaginary news event and act it out.

9. Ask your child to find out all he can about something that interests him, as how a caterpillar becomes a butterfly, what makes a plant grow. Help him locate this information.
10. Play Twenty Questions, or that old favorite, Animal, Vegetable, or Mineral.
11. Have him name as many words as he can beginning with some single letter, or name as many things as he can of a certain color.

As you can see, there is really no end to it. Almost any aspect of living provides opportunities for creative activity, especially when your boy or girl is Six years old.

THE CHILD'S BODY IN ACTION

Even by Five-and-a-half and increasingly at Six, the calm composure so characteristic of Five will be disturbed. Now the boy or girl becomes increasingly restless. The child plays indoors or outdoors and sometimes doesn't seem to know which place he wants to be. He occupies himself outdoors with digging, dancing, climbing. He rides his tricycle (or bicycle) downhill. He carts things about in his wagon. Sand, water, and mud play keep him occupied.

Indoors, household tasks provide many good motor activities. He likes to set the table and help his mother by getting things for her. When asked what he likes to play he may say, "Just one thing after another."

The typical Six-year-old is almost constantly active, even when sitting. (This is one reason that first grade is so difficult for many boys. The sitting requirements imposed by many teachers are just too great.) Even while seated the child wriggles and bounces in his chair, sits on the edge, may even fall off.

He seems to be consciously balancing his body in space. He is everywhere—climbing trees, crawling over, under, and about his large block structures. He seems to be all

legs and arms as he dances about a room, and his coordination is not always good.

He enjoys boisterous, ramble-scramble play. He likes to wrestle with his father or a sibling, but this may end in disaster, for he does not know when to stop. Indoors his ball play may become a menace as he bounces, tosses, and tries to catch. Outdoors he tries stunts on a trapeze bar; likes to pull himself on a rope and swing. Six loves to swing as high as possible.

But he overextends himself in much of his motor behavior. He may not only swing too high, but he likes to build his blocks so high that they may fall.

There are also noticeable changes in the eye-hand behavior of the Five-and-a-half to Six-year-old. Six seems more aware of his hand as a tool, and he experiments with it as such. He is reported to be awkward in performing fine motor tasks, yet he has a new demand for such activities. Tinker Toys and tools are especially intriguing to him. He may be interested less in what he accomplishes with tools than with the mere manipulation of them. He likes to take things apart as well as put them together.

In coloring or printing he is awkward, shifts his body position as well as his grasp of the crayon, and tilts his head. He may stand and lean way over the table and continue to draw, or he may rest his head down on his arm. He often stands or even walks as he works.

There is also a good deal of oral activity as he works: tongue extension and mouthing, blowing through and biting lips. He bites, chews, or taps his pencil. Pencil grasp is less awkward than at Five-and-a-half, but his performance is still laborious.

He touches, handles, and explores everything in sight, but there is often more activity than accomplishment. In carpentry the child needs a good deal of help. His saw bends and gets jammed. He pounds and pounds while driving nails, but often fails to hit them on the head and may even break the board. He may hold his hammer near its head. He can, however, sometimes make crude structures.

So far as *vision* goes, Five was good at making an adequate visual adjustment to some one spot. Six, more expansive, is interested in looking at the world from more than one point of view, in seeing how things relate, in the actual visual process itself. He realizes that there are new combinations to be made, even though he may not always accomplish them successfully.

(This is so typical of Six in many ways. He enjoys the process quite as much as the product, and his products do not always turn out quite the way he expects them to.)

The child of this age seeks to find *relationships.* So we see the beginning of new visual combinations. Six is aware of new objects and new positions in space.

Some children now actually change their eye preference from what it was earlier.

Six may be better at *following* than at looking directly at something. That is, ocular pursuit may be superior to ocular fixation. This may be one reason that the typical

Six-year-old finds that he needs to use his fingers in reading in order to keep his place.

Six can shift his eyes more easily than he could just earlier, and he shifts his regard frequently from the task at hand. He does not concentrate visually as well as he did at Five. So he is easily distracted by things in the environment, and his hands may continue to work as he looks in another direction.

The child of this age tends to be more interested in what he is doing *right now* than with his actual final product. In building a tower of cubes, for instance, he makes a more deliberate, regardful approach than earlier, trying very hard to place each cube accurately. The result may be a less good alignment than he managed when he was Five.

Things are breaking up and changing for him, visually as in so many other respects.

As for teething, this is the year when teeth are very busy. Baby teeth fall out and second teeth come in. There are a good many empty spaces in the mouths of Six-year-olds, and their smiles often reveal large gaps.

By Six years of age the average boy or girl now has erupted lower central incisors and six-year molars; and by Six-and-a-half the majority are erupting their upper central incisors and their lower lateral incisors. Second teeth are really on their way.

# chapter six
# THE CHILD'S MIND

Nowadays the growing child's *mind* has become a matter of major concern to many parents and educators. In fact so much is written about the mind and the so-called cognitive process (thinking) that one might almost get the impression that the mind had been discovered within the past few years.

One might also get the impression that the child's mind is something quite different from his body and that thinking is a quite different sort of activity from the other things that the person does.

Actually, though philosophers have debated for ages the relationship between mind and body, today probably most agree that mind and body are not two separate things, but merely two aspects of one unified whole. And as Dr. Arnold Gesell pointed out as many as fifty years ago, "Mind manifests itself in almost everything the individual does with any part of his body."

We feel that almost everything we have been writing about in this book has told you something about your child's mind. It may seem especially arbitrary to separate the preceding chapter on the child's general interests and abilities from this one on his mind.

However, in deference to today's special interest in the mind and mental activities, and in doing what one can to

promote them, we offer you this chapter which will discuss some of those aspects of a child's behavior which to many seem particularly related to his intellect.

SENSE OF TIME

The Six-year-old is, quite naturally, becoming increasingly able and sophisticated in his understanding of time,

58

and his notion of time sequence is expanding. He does not live in the here and now as much as he did at Five.

In fact, he likes to see things in time sequence and he especially likes to hear about times past. He shows marked interest in hearing about his own and his mother's babyhood, especially about the bad things she did as a child. He penetrates the future by thinking about the sequence of significant holidays and family birthdays. He even likes to hear about ancestors, and has a rudimentary notion of the sequence child/parent/grandparent.

He not only likes to think about holidays but has some idea of the seasons and what each brings.

But the majority still cannot tell time by the clock, and duration of time has little meaning for him. Thus it is not usually effective to tell him that he can play for twenty minutes. Some mark at the end of this amount of time is needed—a bell, a reminder, or possibly that the big hand of the clock will be at a certain place.

He can tell at what hour the family has dinner, at what hour they get up, the time he has to go to school, the time he comes home from school, the times of his favorite television programs. He can tell what grade he is in.

SENSE OF SPACE

The child's space world is now expanding. It now includes *relationships* between home, neighborhood, and the entire community. He is no longer as focal or as "here and now" as he was a year earlier.

Though emotionally Six is the center of his own world, his intellectual interest is expanding to include the sun, moon, planets, the whole world. Thus he is now interested in learning about, or hearing about, children from different countries and what *their* lives are like.

If from a religious background, he may be interested in heaven as being "way up there" and may want to know how you get there.

Some, if very well oriented spatially, may even be able

to tell the points on the compass from a familiar starting point, and most can name nearby streets.

At school he no longer is interested just in his own room but in other rooms in the building, and now the map he draws may include locations of these different rooms.

Six is learning to distinguish his own left from his own right hand, but as a rule still cannot distinguish left and right on another person.

However, it should be remembered that with space, as with time, there are great individual differences from child to child. Some children even at this early age (presumably the right-brained children) may be very well oriented in space even though they may not be well oriented in time. Others (presumably the left-brained children) may be well oriented in time but poorly oriented in space.

And these differences do not necessarily change much with added age. There are some adults who are always spatially well oriented, even in a strange new place. Others could get lost or disoriented in their own hometown.

READING

Many children can now read, especially by Six-and-a-half, though each at his or her own level. They are beginning to develop a reading vocabulary and may even recognize some words out of context. They get their clues from the length of the word, or from the beginning sound or letter.

Many do need to use a marker or to point with their finger as they read, so as not to skip to another line. This should be permitted.

Sixes often can now actually read their own familiar books which, earlier, they merely recited from memory.

They like matching word games. They are beginning to be interested in small as well as capital letters. Some like to pick out letters on a typewriter and to type (simple) words from dictation.

Now reading has reached the stage where much of it is

good enough that specific errors, when they do occur, can be identified. Children sometimes add words for balance. Or they may reverse meaning *(come* for *go, I* for *you).* Or they may substitute words of the same general appearance *(even* for *ever, saw* for *was, house* for *horse).* They like to be supplied words when they get stuck, but this is no time to correct their errors unless their own interpretation throws them off the main theme that they are reading about.

If the child is developing at the usual rate, and reading has not been pushed earlier, when the child was not ready for it, reading is now at least on its way. But if not, *WAIT!!* Children can be pushed into error and a feeling that they are never going to be able to read if too much is required too soon. There are boys who, just as they talked a little later than average, are going to be reading a little later than average.

The typical Six-year-old loves to print, or at least to struggle with printing. Grasping his pencil awkwardly near the tip, tongue often protruding with his effort, he struggles with numbers and letters.

Most can print the whole alphabet and nearly all can print their first name. About half can print their last name as well. Most can use capitals and small letters correctly by Six-and-a-half, though the capitals are easier for them. Fewer than one-quarter can yet *write* any part of their name.

On unlined paper their lines tend to slant up or down, or waver in an up-or-down course. The lowercase letters are often drawn as big as capitals. This suggests that children should be allowed to use all capital letters at Six. Lowercase letters could be added from Six-and-a-half on as they become more aware of them.

Nearly all Sixes can print their numbers from 1 to 11, and nearly half can go all the way to 20. Figures most often reversed are 7, 3, and 9. Numbers tend to be large, labored, and uneven.

ARITHMETIC

Arithmetic ability has improved rather substantially, even within the past six months. Now the child can count to 30 or more, by ones. May overestimate how high he can count when asked. Might reply "A million," "A dillion."

Some can count by tens to 100, and by fives to 50, especially as they move on toward Seven.

In counting objects, as pennies, most can count to 20 and give a correct total. Many add correctly within 10; subtract correctly within 5. Interested in balanced numbers as 2 and 2, 3 and 3. Can use simple measurements as pint and quart.

Can write numbers to 20. Write large, with some numbers bigger than others. Still some confusion of letters and numbers.

Quite a bit of talk as child works. If things asked of him are especially difficult, he's apt to say, "That's easy," "That's simple." Or he may truthfully, when asked how far he can count, say, "Twenty. If I try hard enough." Quite a bit of self-praise, "I'm certainly getting good."

Tend to whisper to selves as they write and some complain, "I'm tired. I'm hot, too."

LANGUAGE AND THOUGHT

Five was a talker and Six is even more so. The child of this age *loves* to talk; he loves conversation; he loves to share his thoughts.

Now he likes not only to add facts to his store of information; he enjoys intellectual exercise such as being able to count or spell. And of course he is very proud of any beginning reading abilities he may have achieved.

According to Piaget, the child is coming to the end of the preoperational stage of thinking in which he still is the center of the world, and anything that moves is alive. He is *approaching* Piaget's stage three (concrete operations) in which children recognize the views of others, know that the shape of a container does not affect the quantity it holds. They can tell that ten marbles in a row are more than eight in a row even if the lengths of the rows are the same.

However, most Sixes are merely on the verge of this stage, and so much lack of logic must still be expected. Six is not quite yet at the Age of Reason.

Many now have good pronunciation and their grammatical construction tends to be fairly accurate. Most can detect their own mistakes and may accept correction.

There is an increasing ability to differentiate fantasy

and reality. But interest in magic remains strong. A child may, for instance, pretend that he is magic—has magic ears. And he definitely believes that the tooth fairy substitutes coins for any teeth he has lost and puts under his pillow.

Belief in Santa remains strong and most, if told by older playmates that he is not real, may fiercely deny this possibility. Santa is still as meaningful to most Sixes as to the little boy who said to his mother, "There really isn't any Santa Claus, is there, Mummy?" His mother said that no, there really wasn't. "That's what I thought," replied the little boy comfortably. "He's just a man dressed up who goes all over the world and comes down the chimney and gives everybody presents."

Belief in God, in most, is not yet wavering. Most, if from a religious background, are quite religious at this age. They like to go to Sunday School. Like to hear about the Little Lord Jesus. Even enjoy the ritual of a not too long church service.

Many think of God as the creator of the whole world and responsible for everything. Prayers are important to many, though the child may still expect them to be answered.

Feelings about death are maturing and becoming much more emotional. In fact, the child may worry that his mother will die and leave him. This worry is exaggerated if at about this time a grandparent or other close relative dies. Is beginning to know about different reasons for death: killing, illness, old age.

There is considerable preoccupation and often quite a lot of questioning about graves, funerals, cemeteries. The notion that death is reversible, that is, that people die but then become alive again, is usually over by this time, having reached its height around Five-and-a-half.

But in spite of all his questioning and interest, the child of this age still tends to think of himself as eternal. Does not connect the idea of death with self.

ETHICAL SENSE

The typical Five-year-old thinks a lot about being good. He means and plans to be good, and is often successful in this intent. But most Fives have a rather limited notion of what goodness and badness actually are. Even at Six, the child's concepts are not yet abstract. Rather, to him, goodness is the specific things his parents require or permit; badness the things they disapprove of or forbid.

Here is our own recording of "Things to Do" (clearly *good* things) and "Things Not to Do" (bad things), dictated by a bright child of this age:

## Things to Do

1. Say "I think you are eating good things today."
2. Pleasant things are lovely to do:
   (a) Eat nicely.
   (b) Always say "Please" and "Thank you."
   (c) Always remember to say "Good morning, good afternoon, good evening."
3. Eat dinner by ourselves without having to be reminded.
4. Keep quiet and answer people when they are talking to you.
5. Keeping clothes clean.
6. Keep watches going—wind them up.
7. Go to bed at 7:30.
8. Wake up at 7:30.
9. When people are breaking things, tell them to stop.

## Things Not to Do

1. Not to say "I am not talking to you."
2. Not to say "Give it to me."
3. Not to say "Give me the biggest piece of anything."

4. Spill crumbs on floor.
   (a) Spill milk or water.
   (b) Get food on hands or faces.
5. Set fires anywhere.
6. Pulling away from someone when they are doing something nice for you.
7. Slamming doors.
8. Don't tear books.
9. Shouldn't keep windows open when it rains.
10. Don't tear clothes.
11. Don't break windows.
12. Don't call people when they are busy.
13. Don't break armchairs.
14. Don't pinch people.

Although certainly any parent of a Six-year-old will, hopefully, both practice and preach good moral standards, he or she should not be too upset if the child now and then takes something that does not belong to him, or tells an untruth, or refuses to take the blame for something undesirable that he has done. Good ethical behavior in many comes much later than Six.

SEX

The relative quiescence about sex, so characteristic of the Five-year-old, often changes at Six. It's fair to say that the typical Six-year-old is a rather sexy individual and one who is interested in sex and its ramifications.

Sex play is quite customary, and suggests the (admittedly immature) sexual appeal of the child of this age. It is our impression that more Six-year-olds than children of other related ages are subjected to sexual molestation or advances by strangers and others.

At any rate, sex play is now much enjoyed by many. Children are interested in and stimulated by exposure to or by others, such as pulling down or taking off pants. This play quite easily elaborates into doctor play and the taking

of rectal temperatures with a crayon or the tip of a pencil. If by Four or after parents take temperatures by mouth rather than taking a rectal temperature, this kind of play might be reduced.

As to babies, most now do know that babies grow inside their mothers. Just how and where they get out is not certain, and there is some question as to whether or not it hurts.

Some now are beginning to wonder how the baby gets started. The location where babies grow (inside the mother) is not enough for some, who appreciate that babies have not always existed—they must be started somehow. Most, if they ask, still accept the idea that the baby comes from a seed.

A very few super-sophisticates may think that the baby gets into a woman's body by being swallowed. A few may know that the seed comes from the father, and a very few may think that father plants his seed by hand. Even a beginning concept of intercourse is beyond most and even those who have been told about this by a friend do not as a rule dwell on it or necessarily believe it.

Probably the majority are still quite naive, like the little girl who told her mother, "I want to grow up to be a mummy but how do you suppose I'll find a husband?"

"Oh, it's not too hard," her mother replied. "You'll grow up and go to high school and maybe to college. And then you'll go to dances and parties and meet some nice boy and he may ask to take you home. That's the start."

"And then I'll say, 'Will you marry me?' "

"No. *He* asks *you*. But he won't ask you right away."

"Oh no, of course not. We'll have to tell each other our names a few times."

Six-year-old girls, in their doll and paper-doll play, may be especially interested in weddings and brides, as well as in families and babies. But their immaturity of concept is evidenced by the fact that perhaps a majority of Six-year-olds still do not connect the enlarged abdomen of the pregnant woman with the presence of a baby inside—even though nearly all now have the concept of the baby growing inside the mother's body.

A few Six-year-olds may experiment with the possibility of having a baby. They may put a doll under their dress and arrange for it to appear, presumably "born." Others play the role of the opposite sex. Boys tuck up their penises and pretend to be girls. Girls tuck their hair up under a cap, dress in what they consider boyish clothing, and demand to be called by a masculine name. This kind of activity in either sex does not as a rule last long.

Things are obviously blossoming at this time. Children are feeling something or other rather strongly. They need help, and calm, unanxious understanding when either their actions or their questions give us clues that they have sex on their minds, at this undoubtedly rather sexy age. (One day, we hope, specialists can tell us just exactly what *is* going on, or at least can tell us more about the level of sex hormones in the child's bloodstream at this time.)

HUMOR

Humor at Six tends not to be very subtle. In fact, it consists for the most part of silly giggling, which can at times be rather tiring to the adult. Interestingly enough, perhaps, a typical Six-year-old may go back to the kind of bathroom humor which Four found so irresistible but which was to a large extent lacking at Five.

So, Six giggles, sometimes uncontrollably, over bathroom words such as "wee-wee" or "pee-pee"; he giggles over "panties," over bathroom situations. And his belly button is again, to him, a very humorous part of the body.

Or a boy may think it tremendously amusing to pretend to "pee-pee" in his mother's lap. A girl may once again, as earlier, pretend to urinate standing up, but now she does it to be humorous and not as an experiment as when she was younger.

Humor may take the form of showing off, especially when there is company. Any silly thing the child may do which calls attention to himself may delight him, tiresome as it may be to adults and embarrassing as it may be to his parents.

But there is one nice aspect of humor seen here much more than it was just earlier. If adult and child are in a special warm mood toward each other, and if the adult is paying full attention to the child, and during this friendly time may make a joke, the child, if intelligent enough to recognize it as such, will be delighted. He may repeat it over and over and may even tell others about this lovely bit of humor.

As always, Six is at his best with the adult if full attention is being paid to him. It is mostly when he feels neglected or shut out that he acts foolish and conspicuous in order to call attention to himself.

# chapter seven
## SCHOOL

So now your Six-year-old boy or girl, simply by being Six, is presumed to be ready for first grade. And this is a step and a half!

Kindergarten, though infinitely more demanding than nursery-school—especially in these unfortunate days when many Five-year-olds are required to learn to read— is still miles from first grade. Any kindly, understanding, and experienced kindergarten teacher, regardless of the demands of the curriculum and the administration, will, hopefully, go a little easy on her pupils.

Not necessarily so with first grade. Here the demands are very definite—and often unrealistic—in spite of what the teacher's instincts might recommend.

"Keep those pencils out of their hands and those workbooks off their desks as long as you can," advised a wise and understanding primary school principal of days long gone. Unfortunately, not all primary school principals today agree. All too many first-grade teachers demand, or are required to demand, unreasonable and unrealistic performance from their pupils.

At any rate, our recommendation for first-graders as for kindergarten boys and girls is that those in charge be certain that before starting first grade a child be not merely

fully Six years old, but that he or she be developmentally up to the demands of first grade.

That is, as for other grades, age alone or even a high intelligence quotient will not guarantee school success. Our basic recommendation with regard to school is that the child be not just old enough chronologically (by law) to theoretically do the work of any given grade. It is not so much the child's birthday, or chronological age, but his *behavior* age that should determine the time he starts kindergarten, and subsequently, the time at which he or she is promoted to first grade.

Quite obviously then, we urge strongly that not all Five-year-olds be automatically entered in kindergarten; not all Six-year-olds be automatically admitted to first grade.

We prefer that if possible every child, before he or she takes that big step from kindergarten to first grade, have the privilege of being given a careful behavior examination.[2,3] The results will indicate his behavior or developmental age—the age at which he (or she) as a total organism is behaving.

Such an examination, when given to any Six-year-old, should indicate clearly whether such a child is fully ready for first grade or is, perhaps, only of a maturity level which would suit him better for a pre–first-grade (or reading readiness) class, or even perhaps, still, only for another year of kindergarten.

However, not every school, as yet, provides somebody qualified to give a behavior examination, and a school psychologist or a psychologist in private practice is not always available. Here then are twelve typical questions selected from a fuller scale of fifty-four in all, offered by John J. Austin in his useful publication *The First Grade Readiness Checklist.*[4]

According to Austin, when the full fifty-four questions are asked, if fifty to fifty-four of these can be answered "Yes," readiness for first grade is reasonably assured. Forty-seven to forty-nine "Yes" answers suggest that readiness is very probable. Below that, readiness is questionable, doubtful, or unlikely.

The twelve typical questions listed here will give you an idea, relatively, of how many "Yes" answers you could give in thinking of your own child:

1. Will your child be six years, six months or older when he begins first grade and starts to receive reading instruction?
2. Does your child have two to five permanent or second teeth?
3. Can your child tell, in such a way that his speech is understood by a school crossing guard or policeman, where he lives?
4. Can he draw and color and stay within the lines of the design being colored?
5. Can he stand on one foot with eyes closed for five to ten seconds?
6. Can he ride a small two-wheel bike without helper wheels?
7. Can he tell left hand from right?
8. Can he travel alone in the neighborhood (four to eight blocks) to store, school, playground, or to a friend's home?
9. Can he be away from you all day without being upset?
10. Can he repeat an eight- to ten-word sentence, if you say it once, as "The boy ran all the way home from the store"?
11. Can he count eight to ten pennies correctly?
12. Does your child try to write or copy letters or numbers?

And if lists are helpful to you, here is our own Gesell list of signs of readiness for first grade. (There is, quite naturally, some overlap in the two lists, since we are talking about the same things.) Failure on a few of our items does not necessarily indicate unreadiness for first grade. But a

significant number of "No" answers should most certainly make you question.

1. Does your child's kindergarten teacher recommend that he go on to first grade?
2. Will he be fully Six or preferably older before the September date when school begins?
3. Does he seem to you as mature as other children his same age?
4. Has the ordinarily "good" behavior of the typical Five broken up a bit and does your child show some signs of being or becoming a rebellious, argumentative Six?
5. Can he copy a circle counterclockwise, starting at the top?

6. Can he copy a triangle?
7. Can he copy a divided rectangle, angled lines crossing the center?
8. Does he hold a pencil in a good two- or three-finger grasp?
9. Can he print at least his first name?
10. Does he know his upper- and lower-case letters out of context?
11. Can he count to thirty?
12. Can he write numbers up to twenty?
13. Does he know his right hand from his left?
14. Does he know his age and the month of his birthday?
15. Can he stand on one foot while you count to eight?
16. Can he throw a ball overhand?
17. Can he tie his shoelaces?
18. Can he repeat four numbers after hearing them once?
19. Can he calculate (add and subtract) within twenty?

Here's a bit more help. Suppose your child has already begun first grade and yet you question his readiness. The following are some of our clues that a boy or girl may not be fully ready for first grade.

Keep in mind that unreadiness for first grade is just as likely to be demonstrated at home as at school. In fact, a prime sign of unreadiness is if the child objects vigorously to going to school, says he hates school, and doesn't want to go.

A little of this "I don't want to go to school today" behavior is not unusual in any child of any age, but when objection to school persists as a daily matter, and when each morning brings a struggle to get the child ready for school and onto the bus, it is obviously a warning sign that something isn't right.

In extreme cases the child may even be sick to his stomach, or unable to eat any breakfast at all. Such a child is not being bad. He is telling you plainly that the situation is too much for him.

Once at school, unready children tend to show a very

short attention span. They are restless. It is hard for them to stay in their seats and they claim that the "work" is too hard. Especially if they are bright, the teacher is likely to complain that "He could do better if he would just try." Toileting accidents, either in school or on the way home from school, are also good clues that too much is being demanded.

If any child is fully ready for first grade when first grade hits him, there is a very good chance that the rest of his schooling may go well, or at least reasonably well. Readiness at this point is so very important that it is well worthwhile to be sure that your child *is* ready.

### HALF-DAY FIRST GRADE

One thing which might help any first-grader, ready or not, would be to shorten the first-grade school day. This is something we have been recommending for years, and many schools have tried it successfully.

Up till now, however, there have been no research results to convince the doubters. Now we can report favorable research. Principal John C. Mulrain of Woodbridge, Connecticut, has, along with Superintendent Alexander M. Raffone, conducted half-day first-grade programs. Recently he checked on the effect of the shortened school day by analyzing the acquisiton of basic skills at the third- and sixth-grade levels of children who *had* experienced the half-day first grade as compared with children in the same school system who had *not* experienced the half-day.

Statistical analysis of data indicate that academically there was no significant difference between the two groups. And 93 percent of the teachers interviewed (teachers who had had two or more years experience with the shortened day) considered that this shortened day resulted in less pupil fatigue; 92 percent felt that it had lessened pupil frustration; 79 percent considered that the children's attention span was improved by a shorter day; 85 percent observed the positive effects of the shortened day in the area of pupil enthusiasm.

As for the parents of these children, 87 percent felt that the shortened day had met the academic needs of their children; 88 percent felt that it had no negative relationship to the child's acquisition of the basic skills; and 82 percent felt that the shorter day met their children's social needs. Eighty-four percent of all parents questioned recommended the continuation of the shorter school day program.

Anyway, it is something important for parents and schools to think about.

# chapter eight
# THE SIX-YEAR-OLD PARTY

The Six-year-old characteristically wants to be first, to be loved most, to receive the exclusive attention of any adult who may be present. He finds it most difficult to wait while somebody else is having a turn. All of this makes him less than an ideal party guest.

Since the Six-year-old is often at his worst with his own mother, any Six-year-old party may proceed more smoothly when the guests' mothers are not on hand.

Six not only wants, he seems to need, always to win. So multiple prize giving is necessary to keep everybody happy. This multiple giving of prizes, especially of a farewell gift for each child, is also important because of the fact that Six is characteristically more of a taker than a giver. Though it is not difficult for the Six-year-old to give a gift to the birthday child, he also wants a present for himself in return. If he himself receives a certain amount of party loot, it will make things easier and more satisfactory for him.

Six is by nature combative and aggressively quarrelsome. When differences of opinion arise in his play with friends, he is prone to "fight it out" in overt physical combat. Thus constant adult supervision is needed at a party to maintain mutual harmony.

Six's emotions are violent and uncontrolled. Sixes at a

party can easily disintegrate either into silly laughter or into hysterical tears. Thus adults in charge will need to be on their toes every minute to prevent chaos. But the Six-year-old loves a party. He anticipates it in advance, relishes it while it lasts, and enjoys it in retrospect. Thus most parents do find the whole venture worthwhile because of the pleasure it gives, in spite of temperamental difficulties which tend to make a party for Six-year-olds hazardous and exhausting for the adults in charge.

KEYS TO SUCCESS

As at Five, the key to success here is good advance planning. However, planning should include the realization that the schedule may not be followed as rigidly as seemed desirable at Five. Definite planned activity is important at the beginning and end of this party, but other plans may need to shift as the party proceeds.

*Number of Guests.* Five guests (plus host or hostess) make an ideal number. Both boys and girls may be included.

*Number of Adults.* Adults at the party should be Mother, Father, and one adult helper; or Mother and two adult helpers. No parents of guests stay—parents bring the children and drop them just outside the house. Most Sixes behave much better when their mothers are not there.

SCHEDULE

Party hours will depend on whether the party is held on a weekend day or on a school day. On a weekend, a lunch party is good—from 1:00 to 3:00 P.M. If the party has to be on a school day, it might be held from 3:30 to 5:30. Two hours is quite long enough.

1:00–1:20    Definite planned activity here is important, but it has to be individual, since all will not arrive at the same time. Children sit at a small table and color, cut, play with pipe cleaners or Plasticine. Host opens presents during this period, and guests watch. But this may not be too orderly. Some hosts will wait till all presents have arrived; others prefer not to. Some may refuse to open presents at this time.

1:20–1:30 Children play games—the same games which they play and like at school. (Find this out from your child in advance.) Good games may be Doggie Doggie Where's Your Bone, Hot Potato, Giant Step.

1:30–2:00 Refreshments. Table, as at other ages, has been set beforehand and is ready in another room. A simple luncheon menu may include carrot sticks, hot dogs and rolls, cake, ice cream, milk. At each place are a paper plate, heavy small glass, napkin, big place card with name lettered in big capital letters, since now most can read their own names and like to do so. There can be a little paper cup at each place with candy in it. Favors—ring, penny, button, thimble, each wrapped in wax paper—may be in the cake. A homemade party hat for each child can be a big feature of the luncheon. There is lots of eating, lots of talk, much interest in hats, in favors, and in each other.

2:00–2:10 Fishing Pond game. Behind a sheet-draped card table, representing the pond, one of the adults or an older sibling puts little presents onto hooks dangled from fishing poles. Children take turns. Suitable gifts for this are: Scotch tape, little pencil sharpeners of special shapes, tape measures, Life Savers, little Indian figures.

2:10–end Some kind of outing if weather permits.

*83*

The length of this will vary some, depending on the kind of outing and the distance to be traveled, so the party might need to last a little longer than the prescribed two hours.

Good places to visit on such an outing include a museum, an animal farm, a nature center, a zoo, a toy-train exhibit. The three adults take the children in two cars. When this trip is over, give each child a final farewell present (as, for instance, a small live turtle), and drop him off at his home.

(If anything happens, as it may, so that you cannot go on this trip, a good substitute activity is a cartoon movie shown at home. In fact, if a projector and film need to be hired, it may be safer to have them on hand anyway. If your planned trip seems to be falling through and you cannot obtain a film and projector, you might fill in this final period by letting the children watch a suitable TV program.)

HINTS AND WARNINGS

Allow some flexibility of schedule but do not allow the children to take over, or things will become a shambles.

This will probably be a very wearing party for the adults in charge. Six-year-olds often act very badly at parties. They can go wild more quickly than children of almost any other age. They tend to do this in a destructive, noisy way. They may pinch, poke, push, fight. Their humor is apt to be aggressive. Their drive toward activity and exploration is tremendous. They are likely to get out of bounds unless well supervised. Their emotions are strong and not well controlled. Don't be surprised if there are tears and trouble. Considerable organization and control on the part of the adult are needed.

The Six-year-old is extremely acquisitive, very egocentric, and a great collector. He may want everything for himself. Other people's things may get into the bag in which he is collecting his toys and favors. Also, host or guests may behave in a self-centered, demanding, unmannerly way not usually considered suitable by adults for either hosts or guests. Solve problems as simply as possible.

# chapter nine
## INDIVIDUALITY

Infants are individuals. So are preschoolers and school-age children. In fact, so are all living human beings. It is important in a book like this for us to stress this obvious fact because of possible misinterpretation.

There are those who believe, incorrectly, that when we describe the typical and characteristic behavior of the child of any age, in this instance the Six-year-old, we are implying that all Sixes behave alike.

We do believe that nearly all children, as they mature, go through very much the same stages and in pretty much the same order as all other children. But their surroundings are all different, and that makes a difference. Perhaps even more important, their personalities are all different, *so that every child goes through the customary stages in his or her own individual way.*

Many students of human behavior have offered their own special classifications or descriptions of the way that human personality differs from one person to another. One of the best-known classifications is that of Dr. Stella Chess of New York University Medical Center. Since her observations[5] fit nicely with our own, we'll summarize here our adaptation of her classification.

*1. Activity Level.* From birth on (in fact, some think even before birth) children differ in the amount of activity they express. If you have more than one child of your own you have noticed this yourself. Some children are always active, always on the go. Even when sitting in a chair, parts of their body are in motion. They are happiest when active. The extreme example of this type is the so-called hyperactive child. It is important not to label a normally very active preschooler or school-age child hyperactive just because he or she moves around a lot.

Others are infinitely more quiet. They may not be particularly interested in physical or athletic activity. In fact, they may prefer no activity at all or may be happiest with their "nose in a book" or just watching television.

2. *Regularity.* Some children are born with what seem like better biological time clocks than others. As infants, if permitted, they put themselves very early on a regular schedule. They are easy to toilet train. As Six-year-olds they may like to do pretty much the same thing every day. They like to have things planned and like to follow the plan.

Others, from infancy onward, are more irregular. As infants they are unpredictable. It is hard to schedule their activities. And as Six-year-olds they continue this unpredictability. It is hard for them to get into the rhythms of daily living. Daily events, such as having to get ready for school in the morning, often seem to come to them as a surprise. They are often hard to manage because one never knows quite what to expect from them.

3. *Adaptability to Change in Routine.* Some children accept a change in schedule very easily. You name it; they like it. As one mother described her middle child, "She is my adventurous eater." Others want the same thing, at the same time, in the same way, day after day, and are very upset by change.

The more adaptable child manages nicely when the family is visiting or even if they have to move to another house or city. The less adaptable may be bothered even by having dinner late, let alone by a visit or a move.

*4. Level of Sensory Threshold.* There are some children (we once personally knew one) who could sleep if a brass band was practicing in the next room. Others will wake with a start if you so much as whisper anywhere in the household. Grandparents sometimes think that such children are spoiled. We think that they are just born that way.

Some react violently to even a small amount of pain. Six-year-olds seem especially vulnerable in this respect. The mere application of nose drops or the braiding of their hair may cause them apparently excruciating pain. Others can accept even a quite severe spanking with apparent equanimity. They just don't seem to feel things the way some others do. It is not that they are braver. They are just less sensitive.

*5. Positive or Negative Mood.* Some children do, unfortunately, seem to have a predominantly negative or complaining mood. It is hard to satisfy them. Things always go wrong for them, or so they think. People and events seldom live up to their expectations. They are almost always unhappy or disappointed. This can be seen especially at Six when the child of that age complains, "*Nothing* ever goes right for me!"

At the opposite extreme are those basically cheerful and happy children who always seem to see the bright side of things. And whether it is because of their attitude or just some quirk of fate, it is true that they do seem to attract good things.

*6. Intensity of Response.* Just as some children feel things more intensely than others do, also some respond more intensely. So in response to the same kind of accident or incident, one child may merely whimper softly whereas another will howl as if the world were coming to an end.

Six in general is given to intensity of response but even at this age there are some children, perhaps those with a very low energy level, who always respond mildly even when angry or upset. One cannot always tell by the loudness of the cry how great the hurt or injury really is.

*7. Distractability.* Some children are highly distractable. The sound of a typewriter, or conversation in the next room, or a branch scratching against a window may make it impossible for such a child to concentrate. The other children, at school or at home, "bother" him by the smallest things they may be doing.

At the other extreme are the nondistractable children. They could work or play, undistracted, even in the middle of a whirlwind. As they grow older, such children actually seem (or so they claim) to be able to study better with radio or even television on than when things are quiet.

*8. Persistency.* Most of you know at least some persistent children who absolutely will not give up till they have finished what they are doing. Since such boys and girls also often tend to be perfectionists, it sometimes seems to parents and teachers as if they never will finish. Persistency, of course, has its good and its bad sides. When the task is something you *want* them to finish, you're glad they stick to it. But when it is something, to you, of minor importance and you want them to get on to something else, this persistency can be highly irritating.

Quite the opposite of the persistent child is the one who lacks persistence. He will leave a stream of half-finished tasks or activities behind him while he goes restlessly searching for something new.

The first can play for hours with some fairly simple play activity. The other seems always to be complaining, "I have nothing to play with, nothing to do."

This, in paraphrase, is Stella Chess's classification of some of the main things a parent may like to look for in a child's personality. A different system of classification, and one which we use consistently, is William Sheldon's system of constitutional psychology.

As we have described in an earlier volume[6] Sheldon's system of constitutional psychology proposes that behavior is a function of structure and that we can, to quite an extent, predict how any child will behave from an observation of what his body is like. Though no individual is *all* one thing or another, there are three main components

that go to make up the human constitution, and in most people one or the other does predominate.

These three components are endomorphy, mesomorphy, and ectomorphy. The body of the endomorph is round and soft; that of the mesomorph hard and square; that of the ectomorph linear, fragile, and delicate.

In the *endomorph,* arms and legs are relatively short as compared with the trunk, with the upper part of the arm longer than the lower part. Hands and feet are small and plump. Fingers are short and tapering. In the *mesomorph,* extremities are large and massive, with upper arm and leg equal to lower arm and leg in length. Hands and wrists are large, fingers squarish. In the *ectomorph,* arms and legs are long compared with the body, the lower arm longer than the upper arm. Hands and feet are slender and fragile, with pointed fingertips.

Recognizing your own child's body type and knowing how endomorphs, mesomorphs, or ectomorphs customarily behave, or are thought to behave, may help you fit your own expectations closer to reality than might otherwise be the case. It is sometimes easier to understand and accept your child's behavior if you believe that he behaves as he does because of the way his body is built than if you think that sometimes less than ideal behavior is either your fault or his.

According to Sheldon, then, the endomorphic individual is one who attends and exercises *in order to eat.* Eating is his primary pleasure. The mesomorph attends and eats *in order to exercise.* What he likes best is athletic activity and competitive action. The ectomorph, on the other hand, exercises (as little as possible), and eats (with indifference) *in order to attend.* Watching, listening, thinking about things, and being aware are his most enjoyable activities.

Another clue to the differences among these three types is that when in trouble the endomorph seeks people, the mesomorph seeks activity, the ectomorph withdraws and prefers to be by himself.

Time orientation, too, is something that may vary with

physical structure. Our experience has been that the endomorph tends to be most interested in the here and now. The mesomorph seems to be forward looking; the next thing or the new thing is what interests him. The ectomorph seems interested in past as well as future.

Since most Six-year-olds are now attending school, it may be useful for parents and teachers alike to know something about the way children of these three main different physical endowments may be expected to behave in a school situation.

*The ectomorph,* being one who often approaches new situations cautiously and even with difficulty, may find adjustment to both kindergarten and first grade difficult. The first days of any school year may be hard for him. Since often, though not always, the ectomorph tends to be immature for his age, it is especially important to be as certain as possible that he is really ready for first grade at the time he enters.

This child, by nature shy, may find that getting used to a new teacher and new ways of doing things is quite difficult. He may feel things deeply—may mind very much if left out or if he doesn't get his proper turn, yet may be too shy to ask for it. A teacher needs to watch very carefully to be sure that the ectomorph is not suffering in silence.

Many ectomorphs seem to do best in a reasonably structured situation. Recess may be harder for them than classroom demands. And the large open classroom with maybe fifty or one hundred children all glumped together may be torture indeed.

However, with his characteristically intellectual approach and his desire to please and conform, especially if he is bright, the ectomorphic child may be among the best students in a class.

*The mesomorph,* especially if a boy, may be the one who has the hardest time in first grade. He is a person of action, and sitting still at a desk, if required, is difficult for him. Also, he tends to be loud and noisy, and this is not always permitted. This child's natural need for activity is often interpreted as badness, and often quite unfair disciplinary measures are taken against a child whose only crime is his own basic personality.

Such children tend to be leaders and are usually very popular with the other children but are all too often in trouble with the authorities.

The round, plump *endomorph* likes people, and is himself (or herself) usually liked by others. Later on, in the older grades, teacher and parents may castigate him for not trying hard enough, not being competitive enough, not caring whether he comes out ahead or not. But in preschool, kindergarten, and first grade the endomorphic boy or girl tends to be both popular and happy. He is casual and easygoing.

THE RIGHT-BRAINED VERSUS THE
LEFT-BRAINED INDIVIDUAL

There is one further way of looking at personality which many parents have found helpful. This is to make an evaluation, which should not be too hard to do, as to whether it is the right side of your child's brain which dominates, or his left.

It is currently accepted that the left cerebral hemisphere governs language functions and verbal communications and the time sense. The right cerebral hemisphere governs visual-spatial configurations and manipulatory performances.

In other words, left-brained children (who are usually right-handed) are often very good at reading, writing, talking—all the things which most schools demand. Often they are very poor at manipulating things and may not be too well oriented in space.

On the other hand, right-brained people (who tend to be left-handed) are often better at manipulating things, at mechanical things, at activities in the three-dimensional world.

Left-brained children can tell or describe; right-brained children can perform.

Our schools for the most part beam their instruction through a left-brained input (reading and listening) and a left-brained output (talking and writing), thereby handicapping the right-brained girl or boy. Educators are now suggesting that schools should try to be fairer to the right-brained child, who may find learning in the usual ways (through reading and being talked to) difficult.

Some parents will perhaps find one of these ways of looking at personality more useful than others. The important thing is to keep one's eyes open and to try to identify your own child's special personality in ways that will help you understand him as an individual, as well as a member of his or her age group.

# chapter ten
## STORIES FROM REAL LIFE

REMAIN CALM

Dear Doctors:

I am beginning to believe that my Six-year-old daughter's problem is me. When she begins crying broken-heartedly and saying she hates herself because she's always bad and never does anything right, I am sad because I realize this must be the way I make her feel.

I have always expected too much from her. Every day I say, "Today I'll be easier on her," but before the day is out I'm harping and prodding and correcting. Of course some of my criticisms are valid, but many are unnecessary.

I have a son Two-and-a-half and now a new baby besides Coralie and I could put the blame on being tired, but there's more to it than that. Perhaps you could suggest some reading about Six-year-olds to help me re-evaluate my expectations of her.

It is quite normal, even though not very nice, for children of Coralie's age to be "all mixed up with" their mothers. And it is also quite typical that the mother blames herself and vows, each day, that today will be better than yesterday.

We think you are blaming yourself too much. At this normally rebellious age (as again at Eleven years when you get the same thing again, only worse) it is important for a mother to divorce herself emotionally as much as she can from her child. Just be as fair and reasonable as you can. And when your daughter starts carrying on, try to remain calm and objective.

(We remember one little girl of this age, criticized by her mother as they were driving along, who wailed convincingly, "Just put me out of the car and leave me here by the side of the road to die!")

But since children of this age tend to be worse with their mothers than with anybody else, try to get somebody else to handle at least some of the routines. (*You need help,* anyway, if you have three children Six and under.)

Many mothers, like you, feel that the trouble with their child is themselves. This may be partly true, but keep in mind that it would also be true if somebody else were your daughter's mother.

Even a few months more time, and school, will help. Also try that miracle solution—time alone with her grandmother. You ask for a book to read—try our own *The Child from Five to Ten* by Gesell, Ilg, and Ames (Harper & Row).

SIX-YEAR-OLD COMPLAINS THAT MOTHER DOESN'T LOVE HIM

Dear Doctors:

My son, Frank, is Six-and-a-half years old. He is a normal child in every way and is also a very good child. He is very affectionate and I think I show him just as much affection in return.

The problem is he says I don't love him. Even when he is just sitting around, all of a sudden he will say, "I love you but you don't love me." I tell him this is not true, but he insists it is.

His dad works away from home most of the time and is just home weekends. I work, too, but we have a wonderful woman who cares for him. Do you think we are not with him enough, or what is wrong? *It hurts me* to have him say these things, although he doesn't seem very sad about it. I mean, he doesn't cry.

Many children like to play this game of "You don't love me,"or "You don't love me enough," or "You don't love me as much as I love you." Grown-ups, too, play it with each other, but to the Six-year-old his mother—not a person of the opposite sex—tends to be the chief object of his affection.

Therefore, feeling as so many do so much of the time that he is not loved as much as he loves, it is quite natural that he makes this complaint. It is natural and reasonable, but you should not take it too seriously.

You can talk with him about it to a certain extent. Tell him this is the way lots of children feel and that usually (and especially in his own case) it is not true. You *do* love him.

But don't let the situation get out of hand. His complaints may become even more frequent when he reaches the suspicious age of Seven, when so many children think their mother doesn't love them, their teacher hates them, their friends are mean to them.

Since you say your son doesn't seem *too* sad when he makes these complaints, chances are he just wants a little special reassurance. Going-to-bed time, with a Six-year-old, is a specially good time for a little snuggling and affectionate talk. In the daytime, when he makes his complaint, just take him on your lap and talk about what a good little boy he is and how glad you are that you have him. Tell him how much you and his dad think of him. Hopefully that should do it.

Above all, try not to feel hurt that he talks this way. It is, with most children, just a part of growing up.

LITTLE BOY'S INSECURITY, MARKED JEALOUSY
OF YOUNGER SISTER, DISTURBS MOTHER

Dear Doctors Ilg and Ames:
I have two children, a girl Three and a boy Six. The

boy is extremely jealous. He is a boy I can be proud of, no matter where I take him. But he has developed a complex and is convinced that nobody loves him. He says I love his sister more than I do him and asks why did I have him if I didn't want him. Many a night I have to go to bed with him to quiet him, because he becomes almost hysterical. It seems to help at such times if I tell him about when he was a baby, about how cute he was and all.

He will start school in the fall. I hope things will straighten out. I've avoided nursery school because of finances and also because when the two are separated they are lost. Neither knows what to do without the other.

Your son's behavior is, of course, distressing to you. There seem to be two paths, either of which you can follow. One, and we doubt that this is necessary yet, is to feel that he is seriously unhappy and to try to get psychological help for him. If things don't improve after school starts, you might try this.

The other course, which we would be inclined to follow at this time, is this: Give your son just as much sympathy as you can manage, especially, as you have been doing, at bedtime. But go only so far with it.

Possibly you are being a little too passive. A little more planning—time for him alone with you, time with friends, and separation of him and his sister—could result in his feeling more secure.

MOTHER DOES NOT BELIEVE NORMAL CHILD
PROFESSES HATE FOR PARENTS

Dear Doctors:

I write this letter in a fit of anger, which has lasted for three days ever since I read your miserable column. I presume that for the most part you write about normal children. Well! I don't think you'll find two more normal children in this world than my adorable Six- and Eight-year-old girls. I must keep after them constantly to keep toys and clothes picked up, but by damn! The day will never come when either of them would dare to retort "I hate you" to me or my husband.

The trouble with what you call normal children is parents and doctors like yourselves who write such obnoxious columns. I place all the blame on columns like yours.

My method of raising children certainly seems far more successful than the methods urged by such people as yourselves which I consider ridiculous.

It would be interesting to know just why you went into such a rage. We weren't recommending that children say "I hate you" to their parents. We were simply reporting that they often do.

Just last week a perfectly calm mother wrote to report, without rage, that her son left notes around the house announcing "I love you, Mummy" or "I hate Mummy," depending on how his day had gone.

A young child's emotions are closely tied up with his mother. He loves her most—but when things go wrong he hates her the most, too.

In bygone days, when discipline was stricter, children might not have dared to say "I hate you" out loud. But we remember what some of them muttered.

True, some families are so bland or some mothers so much in control that their children don't shout or even mutter "I hate you." But we imagine, if they're normally spunky, that they think it from time to time.

CHILD TICS WHEN VIEWING TELEVISION

Dear Doctors Ilg and Ames:

My trouble is my daughter Doris, who is just Six. She has developed nervous habits or tics. She makes faces, opens her eyes wide, and at the same time opens her

*101*

mouth as though she's stretching her eyes open. She also turns her head to the side a couple of times. All these actions take place almost solely when watching TV, which I have cut down to three-quarters of an hour per day. She used to watch steadily for three hours or more. I have been reprimanding her quite a lot lately, as she is always doing something she shouldn't—teasing the dog or bird, or else she says she won't do this and that.

I have been thinking of going to the doctor, but there wouldn't be anything to show him as it's seldom done without TV around. I've also thought of having her eyes tested. Just now I'm having all I can do to control myself and not spank her. She went to bed at 7:15. She has had three drinks of water and is clearing her throat continually, saying she has a frog in there. She had me come in two times to give her a kiss, and she wants another drink. It is now 9:15. What shall I do? An Awful Mother.

One bit of encouragement we can give you is that your daughter Doris is going through a typical but excessive Six-year-old phase. The presence of these tensional outlets is, however, telling you a great deal about Doris, because when tensions get too much for her at a later age she will probably express them in similar ways.

Just being Six is often hard enough. Sometimes the additional environmental pressures, such as first grade, make things worse. Fortunately, Doris is still in kindergarten. You have recognized the relationship between her ticking and TV. Could you try disconnecting the set entirely for a week and substituting a good hour's play period with her each day? Parents often don't realize how little "good" time they spend with their children.

As to bedtime, do you chat with her for a few minutes after she is in bed and the lights are out? There are so many things on a Six-year-old's mind, things that need to be talked over and things that don't come to mind until bedtime.

As you learn to realize that a Six-year-old needs to be

handled both with a loose and a tight rein, you will feel more in control, more sure of yourself as a mother. There will be times when you will ignore her defiance and refusals, and other times when you will make certain demands without flinching or giving in. A child is happier when you have a surer hand. And she will tell you by her tensional outlets, or lack of them, whether you are making the right decisions.

CHEWING ON THINGS A COMMON NERVOUS HABIT

Dear Doctors:

I would like your advice as to what course to follow with my Six-and-a-half-year-old daughter, Andrea, who chews gloves, collars, and scarves and almost anything that comes close to her face.

She rarely bites her nails, but is a thumb sucker of long standing. She chews the corner of a blanket while sucking. This is now confined to bedtime mostly, but I am sure the blanket would be dragged around all day if I permitted. She can chew out three glove fingers just on one bus ride to school.

Andrea is the oldest of four children. She is hyperactive, enthusiastic, and compliant. She responds very readily to my attitude—is upset if I am upset or angry with her. Emotionally and temperamentally she is *my* child, and contrary to popular belief, I tend to excuse her faults because I see the same ones in myself.

She is popular, loves school and her teachers, is interested in everything.

Am I right in believing that this chewing is a nervous habit? I try not to nag about it—simply express my disapproval with such instructions as "Don't chew *my* scarf," etc. She doesn't seem under undue pressure at school or at home.

You are quite right that Andrea's chewing on things is a normal nervous habit, or as we usually term it, a "tensional outlet."

Chewing on ribbons, belts, gloves, the ends of braids is extremely common around Six years of age and usually diminishes somewhat as the child moves on toward Seven or Eight. You say that Andrea has always been a thumb and blanket sucker, so clearly this is the type of relief she seeks from tension.

You are right not to nag her about it. Nagging only makes things worse. You are also sensible to make specific prohibitions as, "Don't chew *my* scarf."

Have you ever tried letting her chew gum? (Not an attractive habit, but sometimes this gets a child away from gloves and scarves.) Sometimes it seems more acceptable to see a child chewing or sucking on food than on clothing.

In fact, sometimes you can try substituting snacks for articles of clothing. When you see her chewing, offer raisins, carrot sticks, popcorn—any type of food that will keep her mouth busy for a while.

You will have to use your ingenuity, exercise your patience, and, so far as you can, try to keep her out of tension-producing situations.

As you suggest, being the oldest of four, at her age, means that she has been living in a rather highly charged (we imagine) atmosphere. She probably needs some outlet.

### CHILD WHO IS POOR LOSER AT PLAY MAY NOT BE READY FOR COMPETITION

Dear Doctors:

My Six-year-old is the worst sport in the world. I don't mind a child's not being perfect and I think I am very tolerant with Andrew's lacks in certain departments. But one thing my husband and I can't stand is a poor sport.

We've felt this about Andrew for some time, but we noticed it especially on his birthday. We could hardly help but notice. Andrew received quite a few games, the kind where you move counters on the board to see who can get "home" first.

Andrew and his Eight-year-old sister tried several of these, but none of them worked because he was so horrible. Every time she got the least bit ahead he would cry and rage and accuse her (sometimes justly, often not) of cheating. But whenever he thought nobody was looking, he would push his counters ahead.

We finally couldn't stand him any longer and took the games away and said he couldn't play till he could behave better. But how can we go about teaching him a sense of fairness and a spirit of fair play?

You were right to take the games away for a while. Like most Sixes, Andrew isn't ready for any prolonged competitive play—certainly not with people older and smarter than he.

But don't despair. Being a good sport and a cheerful loser isn't easy, even for some adults. It's virtually impossible for the average Six-year-old.

To lose with a smile requires first of all that you do not care too terribly about the game—and that you must be able to take a back seat once in a while.

The ordinary Six-year-old has neither of these abilities. His emotions are violent and he cares intensely about almost everything. It is almost impossible for him to take a back seat. One of the cardinal rules in his life is that he wants and needs to be first.

Bold and loud as he may be at times, his sense of self isn't secure. Inability to admit wrongdoing and to lose at competitive games are striking aspects of typical Six-year-old immaturity. Protect Andrew when you can from playing competitive games with children who play better than he does. And if you play with him yourself, keep the sessions short and try to see to it (even if you have to cheat a little yourself) that he wins at least part of the time.

IS PASSIONATE FRIENDSHIP UNUSUAL FOR SIX-YEAR-OLD?

Dear Doctors:

I am writing about my Six-year-old granddaughter,

Trixie. She has a little classmate named Arthur as a boyfriend. She wants to be constantly with him, stays at the window watching for him, and wants to call him on the phone to come over to play. She insists on kissing him.

Her father hasn't been very lovable to her. He doesn't hug her or kiss her and doesn't like to have her kiss him. Do you think her behavior with this little boy is unusual for a girl of her age? (Trixie knows I am writing to you.)

I tell her mother that now is the time to handle this situation before Trixie gets older. But Trixie told her mother she didn't want to wait till she was fifty or sixty before she had a boyfriend. She wants one now.

It isn't unusual for a child of Six to have a strong, passionate friendship with some other child and to want to be constantly with him or her. In fact, parents often get extremely fed up with the special friend, who seems sometimes to be the center of their own child's universe.

Children often seem almost spellbound by these friends and will do almost anything they say. It is usually not anything to worry too much about.

However, unless it's necessary for Trixie to phone this little boy to make some special arrangement, now is as good a time as any for her to learn that in our present culture, *girls do best not to call boys.* Also, extreme demonstrations of physical affection should be discouraged.

It is, of course, quite possible that Trixie may be a bit starved for expressions of physical affection. But at this age it's better to be kissing family than friends.

We wouldn't say that Trixie's behavior is "unusual." But we would discourage both the kissing and the phoning. There's no reason, however, why she shouldn't play with Arthur. But perhaps a bit more supervision as well as a bit more inhibition is needed.

And at any age before the teens we try to avoid too much family talk about "boyfriends" and "girl friends." Usually if adults in the family don't carry on in these terms, children won't stress them either. If you could get the term "boyfriend" out of her vocabulary you might help her to see Arthur simply as a special friend and playmate rather than in a more romantic light.

LET SIX-YEAR-OLD CHOOSE HER OWN OUTFIT
IF SHE IS DIFFICULT TO SATISFY

Dear Doctors:

I have just gotten my Six-year-old daughter off to school after our usual morning bout over clothes. She seems unusually sensitive to the feel of clothing and manages to find something that bothers her in almost every outfit she owns. Things are too tight, too loose, too warm, too itchy. Bumps in her socks hurt her feet.

I've tried to be patient, but some mornings when we are on about her fourth dress and fourth pair of socks and the clock is fast approaching school time, I'm ready to explode. Getting up earlier doesn't help; just gives her longer to fuss. Is this behavior common, and what if anything can I do about it?

Your daughter's preoccupation with the fit and feel of things is trying—but we can assure you that this sensitivity usually reaches its peak at Six or Seven and then tapers off. *You* should remember that things probably do feel wrong to her, and try to adapt within reason. But *she* must realize that you can't be pushed beyond a certain point—and that she'll have to leave the house, clothed, eventually, like it or not.

Many mothers find this sensitivity is at its worst when the child is in a tense situation. So you might try to keep things as smooth as possible.

Fortunately, at Six, your daughter is in control of a number of factors. She can tie laces, sashes, and the like so that they feel right to her. If it's a matter of texture, you can let her select from two or even three outfits the one which is least uncomfortable.

Since all of this seems combined with getting her to school in the morning, you may find, as other mothers have, that, cruel as it may seem, you get along better if you step aside and make her responsible for getting herself to school on time. It is heartbreaking to see your own child scuttling over back lots and through shortcuts trying desperately to make up time she's lost fussing and fooling around. But sometimes it is the only way. And once she realizes it's up to her to make it out of the house and to school on time, things may improve considerably.

You can call her in time, have the clothes laid out and breakfast ready, and remind her when she needs reminding. But let her know by your emotional attitude that it's *her* problem.

There may be no ideal solution. But the most successful attitude seems to be one which combines real sympathy with the child's feelings with a certain toughness which makes her know that you will only be pushed so far.

MESOMORPHIC CHILD NEEDS SUPERVISION
ALMOST CONSTANTLY THROUGHOUT THE DAY

Dear Doctors Ilg and Ames:

Our problem is our Six-year-old, Timmy. Timmy is uncooperative, destructive, and downright mean to his younger brother. He deliberately breaks his toys and tears up our mail. Within a month after Christmas he had most of his toys broken and had started on his brother's things. He has ruined a good chair by ripping the fabric on it, and he runs his outdoor things—tricycle, scooter—into things and ruins them. Sent to his room for misbehaving, he drew all over the wallpaper in his bedroom with crayon, then he went into the bathroom and pulled a hook off the wall, including the plaster. Then he got into the closet and pulled clothes and toys all over the floor.

Now for his plus side. He can be very sweet and helpful if he thinks he'll get something for it. He is charming to other people.

He has such boundless energy that I cannot keep my eye on him all the time and can't keep him occupied positively every minute. His kindergarten teacher says he is doing well.

He nearly lost two fingers by holding his hand around the pulley belt on our garden tractor. It wasn't the first time I had to rush him to the doctor or hospital because he couldn't keep his hands off things.

He makes me so mad sometimes I can't see straight. Even my husband, a most patient person, is getting fed up. We both know that Timmy needs a lot of loving, but how do you love a child who does everything he can think of to do wrong? I have lost more sleep over him, cried more tears over him, and still haven't come up with any solution. I know I need professional help but I can't afford it.

A child like your Timmy is very hard on parents, even though you have to admire his tremendous energy and ingenuity and realize that it speaks well for possible future accomplishments. The thing, of course, is how can you yourself hold up until he matures and gets himself in hand.

Your son sounds as though he is of a definitely meso-morphic physique, and his present age just makes things worse. (We have described the mesomorphic individual in the preceding chapter.)

We are glad that Timmy is in kindergarten—that must help some. However, you need more help and more relief than just kindergarten. With children like this it is partly a matter of keeping them occupied in positive, acceptable ways; partly a matter of almost constant supervision. It is also a matter of getting the child away from you for even an hour at a time so you can get your strength back to cope with him when you take him on again.

Much less expensive than professional advice, and possibly equally beneficial, would be to hire a good baby-sitter, preferably a strong, male sitter, who can take your boy on excursions and who can keep him occupied in good, vigorous, physical ways. Also remember that two is company, three is a crowd. Time spent alone with either you or his father may be far more valuable for Timmy than keeping the family unit always together.

KEEPING SIX-YEAR-OLD BOY BUSY
SEEMS BEST WAY TO ASSURE HIS HAPPINESS

Dear Doctors:
What to do with a discontented Six-year-old! Adam is Six and seems to have a terrible case of "want-its." He seems to feel that if he has this or that thing right now, he will be happy. Of course for a while he is content, but then it's something else. He has more toys than any other child on the block and yet when he has to play alone or with his Three-and-a-half-year-old sister the usual lament is, "What can I do now?" He is happiest when doing actual work. He's been allowed to use the electric lawnmower (under supervision), the floor polisher, etc. Those seem to be his happiest moments, but naturally those times are limited.

If I could just get across to him that material possessions don't necessarily make happiness. Is it possible to teach this to a child? Is it possible that this tendency is inherited? I must admit my own childhood was similar in many respects.

There seem to be at least two possibilities about Adam and his present discontent. His need for things to be done or to be available right now does seem a little immature and suggests that he may need to be treated like a somewhat younger child.

On the other hand, the fact that he is happiest when doing actual work suggests that he may be one of the many children who are born workers and not players. Also it is true that many Six-year-olds do like very much to help their mother or father. Apparently the secret is to keep him busy. Of course it is true that that can be as much work for the adult as actually playing with him. But if you and your husband and if possible some older relative or a baby-sitter can plan to do work with him, that may get him through the days.

The fact that he has more toys than any other kid on the block suggests that perhaps you have been a little remiss. Instead of helping him play and behave creatively, you may have just handed him another toy. Some children, often quite bright ones, seem to need to be taught how to play—they aren't creative on their own.

So far as trying to get across to him the fact that material possessions don't necessarily bring happiness—it is too soon to expect much there. This is a rather difficult concept (never grasped by some) and is certainly over the heads of most Six-year-olds.

You note that in many ways he is like you as a child. Certainly temperament can be inherited, at least to a certain extent.

DAUGHTER IS MESSY AND MISPLACES THINGS

Dear Doctors:

My Six-and-a-half-year-old daughter, Felicia, is driving me to distraction. She is a messer. Her bedroom is a disgrace and she takes little pride in her possessions. Never makes her bed. Junk and undressed dolls are strewn from one end of her room to the other. New toys and games get the same treatment.

She loses money and "jewelry" and seems to have no sense of responsibility. She is belligerent when I correct her and will do nothing without detailed instruction. In the morning, she will not toilet, wash, scrub teeth, brush hair without an operation-to-operation instruction. Sometimes it's noon before we get these things done.

When school starts again in the fall I suppose we'll have to get up about 4:00 A.M. to get all this done.

Her kindergarten teacher said she was smart enough and she loves to read; in fact, she is rarely without a book. She calls them her friends. She has few other friends because she is so shy.

These girls who are bright and good readers are often the very ones who have the most difficulty in handling practical, everyday life situations.

We're afraid her difficulties may continue for some time. It may take a very strong stimulus—such as criticism from a much-loved teacher or later from a boy or girl friend—before she will really get down to business.

As to losing things, you're going to have to give her lots of practical help. Mittens or gloves can be fastened to her coat as you do with a younger child.

As to money, don't let her have any large sums. Most Six-year-olds lose their pocketbooks. "Well, where did you leave it?" is a constant refrain of mothers of Sixes when they're downtown shopping together. So if she must have pocketbooks, at least see that they don't contain anything too valuable or expensive. Name tapes in clothes help, where school is concerned.

But in the meantime, till improvement comes, you have to live with Felicia. You have to know where to give in, where to use humor, where firmness. For a while you may have to restrict her major toileting to nighttime. In the morning just see that her hair is combed and that she gets dressed and fed. Other details may have to be put off till nighttime.

Straighten up her room yourself to a passable degree. Have her help you make the bed and reorder and organize her room once a week, probably on Saturday. It isn't so bad when you work together. Your daughter will be quite a lot older than Six before her room is really neat.

Some kind of reward system such as stars, books, or some really big thing may help. But whatever you do, with girls like this, messiness tends to last for quite a long time and you just have to live with it as best you can.

IT IS NOT UNUSUAL FOR A SIX-YEAR-OLD BOY
TO PREFER PLAYING WITH GIRLS

Dear Doctors:

My husband and I just finished a heated discussion about a serious problem. Our son, Peter, aged Six, has girlish tendencies. He is more than fond of dancing and singing. One day he asked his sister if he could put on one of her costumes while he danced. I said he couldn't, so then he asked, "Can I just wear the beads?"

He much prefers to play with girls. I've seen him leave boys of his own age to go and play with little girls. He talks a lot about long hair, pretty hair, pretty dresses. He did learn to ride his two-wheeler when he was only four. And he is intelligent. He has one special love—automobiles. He can name each kind.

This evening he received his last warning about playing with girls. His father said the next time he would spank him very hard. The other boys his age call him sissy; and yet he does sometimes play with them and gets along with them.

Are we handling him correctly? What else can we do to curb Peter's effeminate ways?

This common problem is extremely distressing to parents, especially to fathers. So it's important not to take violent issue with your husband even though you may not approve of his specific methods of handling Peter's behavior.

At least half the time it turns out that parents don't have too much to worry about. Probably a good half of the boys who do seem a little feminine, who are interested in lipstick, flowers, girls' toys and clothes, and in playing with girls, take a turn for the more masculine by the time they are Nine or so. All outward traces of this earlier tendency and interest often disappear, and you wonder why you worried.

Preferring girls as playmates is very common in boys around the age of Six. And although boys like yours may remain more sensitive than the average masculine type, many of these boys turn out to be perfectly "normal," masculine men.

Then there are those who don't take this turn toward the more masculine. Even with this latter, smaller group, discipline and opposition don't have much effect. You can spank them till your hands are tired and completely prevent them from playing with girls. It changes neither their temperament nor their interests.

Therefore, though we would make reasonable efforts to arrange for Peter to play with boys, we would neither prevent him from playing with girls nor punish him for doing so. It's the way he feels, really, rather than what he does, that worries you. Punishment won't change his feelings.

Since his love of girls is balanced by his interest in automobiles, and since his early mastery of a two-wheeler speaks well for his motor coordination, we suspect you may not have anything serious to worry about. Perhaps his father can find more time to play with him. We'd try to cut down on play with girls, if you wish to do that, by providing other interests and activities rather than by punishing.

WHAT A MOTHER CAN DO TO PREVENT
EMBARRASSING ACCIDENTS

Dear Doctors:

I have a terrible, and embarrassing, problem and absolutely no idea what to do. My Six-and-a-half-year-old son, Duncan, is in an enriched first-grade class. That's all very fine, but about a month after he started school he began having toilet accidents on his way home from school.

At first I was horrified and raved and ranted like a mad woman, and, of course, punished him severely. But gradually I began to realize that scolding and punishment were not the answer so I consulted our doctor.

He said the problem was not physical but went deeper than that—and suggested that we consult a child psychologist. Did you ever hear of such behavior in a Six-year-old? And do you think that Duncan needs psychological help. Or what?

We *have* heard of such behavior. It isn't too common, but when it does occur it seems to be most often with a Six-year-old boy. And we doubt that Duncan needs the special help of a child psychologist.

Most mothers, when they run into this problem, react as you did. They get awfully mad. And disgusted. But gradually they begin to realize that the child can't help himself.

You were wise to take Duncan to the doctor to rule out the possibility of anything really physically wrong. It would do no harm, now, to try a child psychologist but we doubt that it's necessary.

First of all, since these accidents have occurred since he has been in first grade, check to be absolutely sure that the demands of school aren't too much for him. He seems fully old enough for first grade, but the demands of the enriched class may be too much.

Second, try to see if he can't function at home before he goes to school. If that doesn't work, perhaps the teacher would help you by having him go to the bathroom before he leaves the school building. If that doesn't work, try calling for him at school, if you can, and driving him quickly home and sending him to the bathroom before he goes out to play.

Often these boys can't function on the toilet at home in the morning, and refuse to use the school toilet. Then, suddenly, on their way home from school, either at noon or more often in the afternoon, they just can't control the sphincter action.

Sometimes we suggest to mothers that they pick their son up after the morning session and take him home to function on his own toilet. All of this supports our feeling that if Sixes had only a half day of school, this kind of problem, and other problems caused by overfatigue and overdemand, just might not occur.

SPECIAL SUPERVISION FROM GROWN-UPS
NEEDED FOR THIS BOY

Dear Doctors:

I have a serious problem with my son who is Six years old. We moved recently and he became friendly with a boy of his own age. Now we have found them repeatedly with their clothes off. This has involved others too, but always these two are involved. When they are separated it doesn't happen. We have punished but to no avail. We have come to the conclusion that it must be one or the other starting it, but which one? Can you help us? We feel that we need professional advice.

The first thing to keep in mind is that this is a very common behavior and not necessarily a sign that anything is wrong. A second thing is to recognize that it really doesn't matter which of the two boys *starts* the behavior. Sex play involves two (or more) people and usually neither one is wholly responsible.

Sex play often occurs in children who may be highly driven sexually. It equally often occurs among children who can't think of anything better to do. We find high points for this kind of behavior around Four years and again at Six.

With some children this kind of play is rather occasional and incidental and can be discouraged easily. With others it seems to be a very strong drive and no amount of punishment or exacting promises does much good. You just have to supervise such children, or forbid them each other's company.

But in doing this, it is important not to give them the idea that sex is bad. You just let them know you don't favor this kind of play, and that there are other interesting things to do.

Sometimes it is hard to supervise directly. But at least have them play in clear open areas. Avoid closed doors and small, isolated places. Then if this kind of play still takes place, separate your son and his friend and say they can't play together for a week (or whatever time you decide on). If you are firm and stick to your plan, in most cases you can more or less put an end to this kind of behavior.

# EPILOGUE

Nobody, but nobody, will ever be as much fun or as much trouble to you as your lively, lovely, difficult Six-year-old.

As earlier, at Two-and-a-half, you may have found his most difficult characteristic to be his tendency to go to opposite extremes. He loves you one minute, hates you the next. He loves to play games with you, but he hates to lose. At times he seems bold and brash, and at others he is such a pushover for just the right technique that he can be almost putty in your hands.

He worries that you won't be there when he gets home from school, yet you and he may be in a tangle as soon as he arrives.

The biggest difference that you will have noticed between your Five- and your Six-year-old is that to Five you were the center of the universe. Six is that center himself.

Looking back, as your boy or girl moves on into the calmer waters of Six-and-a-half and Seven, you will in all likelihood forget the tangles and the tussles, and remember the big-eyed enthusiasm, the eagerness for new experiences and new information, the warm expressions of affection, and the delight in shared experiences.

# APPENDIXES
## Good Toys
## for Six-Year-Olds

The typical Six-year-old is a very active individual, but also very social. He is especially eager to perfect skills which will give him status in his group. Toys are becoming less important than the paraphernalia of sports and games. But he still enjoys some of his Five-year-old playthings.[7]

Airplanes
Anagrams
Balls
Baseball equipment
Beads
Board games
Boats
Cameras, simple
    (Instamatic)
Card games
Chinese checkers
Crafts involving
    small muscle coordi-
    nation (loop looms,
    spool knitting)
Craft materials,
    moderately advanced

Crayons
Croquet set
Doctor and nurse
    accessories
Dolls
Doll accessories and
    clothes
Dollhouse with furniture
Dominoes
Drawing materials
Dress-up materials
Electric train
Field glasses
Fishing tackle
Flashlight
Garden tools, simple
Gyroscope

Ice skates
Jacks
Jigsaw puzzles
Jump rope
Kites
Marbles
Marionettes
Miniature forts, filling stations, farms
Modeling materials that dry or bake to a permanent finish
Paints
Paper dolls
Pedometer

Roller skates
Science materials (magnet, magnifying glass, stethoscope)
Simple erector sets
Stilts
Swing
Tops
Toy soldiers
Trains with tracks, switches, signals
Two-wheel bicycle
War game material
Wheel toys
Workbench and tools

# Books for Six-Year-Olds

Alexander, Martha. *And My Mean Old Mother Will Be Sorry, Blackboard Bear.* (Paperback) New York: Dial, 1977.

Boden, Alice. *The Field of Buttercups.* New York: Walck, 1974.

Borach, Barbara. *Gooney.* New York: Harper & Row, 1968.

Brown, David, *Someone Always Needs a Policeman.* New York: Simon & Schuster, 1972.

Carle, Eric. *The Grouchy Ladybug.* New York: Crowell, 1977.

Carroll, Lewis. *Jabberwocky.* New York: Warne, 1977.

Clifton, Lucille. *My Brother Fine with Me.* New York: Holt, Rinehart & Winston, 1975.

Duvoisin, Roger. *Crocus.* New York: Knopf, 1977.

―――. *Jasmine.* New York: Knopf, 1973.

―――. *Petunia's Treasure.* New York: Knopf, 1975.

Emberly, Ed. *Drawing Book of Faces.* Boston: Little, Brown, 1975.

―――. *Klippity Klop.* Boston: Little, Brown, 1974.

French, Fiona. *City of Gold.* New York: Walck, 1977.

Garland, Sarah. *The Joss Bird.* New York: Scribner, 1975.

Grollman, Earl. *Talking About Death.* Boston: Beacon Press, 1970.

Hurd, Edith Thatcher. *The Mother Owl.* Boston: Little, Brown, 1974.

Jarrell, Randall. *Snow White and the Seven Dwarfs.* New York: Farrar, Straus & Giroux, 1973.

Jewell, Nancy. *Cheer Up, Pig!* New York: Harper & Row, 1975.

———. *Try and Catch Me.* New York: Harper & Row, 1972.

Keller, Charles and Baker, Richard. *The Star Spangled Banana and Other Revolutionary Riddles.* Englewood Cliffs, N.J.: Prentice-Hall, 1974.

Kellogg, Steven. *The Mystry of the Missing Red Mittens.* (Paperback) New York: Dial, 1977.

Kraus, Robert. *Kittens for Nothing.* New York: Windmill, 1977.

———. *My Son the Mouse.* (Paperback) New York: Windmill, 1977.

———. *The Little Giant.* New York: Windmill, 1977.

Kuskin, Karla. *What Did You Bring Me?* New York: Harper & Row, 1973.

Lionni, Leo. *The Greentail Mouse.* New York: Pantheon, 1973.

Mayle, Peter. *Where Did I Come From?* New York: Lyle Stuart, 1973.

Miller, Edna. *Mousekin Takes A Trip.* Englewood Cliffs, N.J.: Prentice-Hall, 1976.

———. *Mousekin's Woodland Birthday.* New York: Collins World, 1974.

Nye, Loyal. *What Color Am I?* New York: Abingdon Press, 1977.

Pinkwater, Manus. *Around Fred's Bed.* Englewood Cliffs, N.J.: Prentice-Hall, 1976.

Richelson, Geraldine. *What Is a Child?* New York: A Harlan Quist Book, n.d.

———. *What Is a Grown-up?* New York: A Harlan Quist Book, n.d.

Schweninger, Ann. *The Hunt for Rabbit's Galoshes.* New York: Doubleday, 1976.

Silverstein, Shel. *The Missing Piece.* New York: Harper & Row, 1976.

Steadman, Ralph. *The Bridge.* New York: Collins World, 1975.

Supraner, Robyn. *It's Not Fair.* New York: Warner, 1976.

Tobias, Toby. *Moving Day.* New York: Knopf, 1976.

Zimelman, Nathan. *Walls Are to Be Walked.* New York: Dutton, 1977.

Zindel, Paul. *I Love My Mother.* New York: Harper & Row, 1975.

Zion, Gene. *The Plant Sitter.* New York: Harper & Row, 1959.

Zolotow, Charlotte. *Do You Know What I'll Do?* New York: Harper & Row, 1958.

———. *When the Wind Stops.* New York: Harper & Row, 1975.

# Books for the Parents
## of Six-Year-Olds

Ames, Louise Bates. *Parents Ask.* A syndicated daily newspaper column. New Haven, Conn.: Gesell Institute, 1952–.
———. *Child Care and Development.* Philadelphia: Lippincott, rev. ed., 1978.
———. *Is Your Child in the Wrong Grade?* New York: Programs for Education, 1978.
———, and Ilg, Frances L. *Your Five-Year-Old.* New York: Delacorte, 1979
Beekman, Daniel. *The Mechanical Baby: A Popular History of the Theory and Practice of Child Raising.* New York: Lawrence Hill & Co., 1977.
Benning, Lee. *How to Bring up a Child without Spending a Fortune.* New York: McKay, 1975.
Braga, Laurie, and Braga, Joseph. *Learning and Growing: A Guide to Child Development.* Englewood Cliffs, N.J.: Prentice-Hall, 1975.
Brazleton, T. Berry. *Doctor and Child.* New York: Delacorte, 1976.
Briggs, Dorothy Corkille. *Your Child's Self-Esteem.* New York: Doubleday, 1970.
Caplan, Frank, and Caplan, Theresa. *The Power of Play.* New York: Doubleday, 1973.
———. *Parents' Yellow Pages.* New York: Anchor Books, 1978.

Coffin, Patricia. *1, 2, 3, 4, 5, 6. How to Understand and Enjoy the Years That Count.* New York: Macmillan, 1972.

Collier, Herbert. *The Psychology of Twins.* Phoenix, Ariz.: Twins, 1972.

Comer, James P., and Pouissaint, Alvin F. *Black Child Care: How to Bring up a Healthy Black Child in America.* New York: Simon & Schuster, 1975.

DeRosis, Helen. *Parent Power Child Power.* New York: McGraw-Hill, 1975.

Dodson, Fitzhugh. *How to Parent.* Los Angeles: Nash, 1970.

———. *How to Father.* Los Angeles: Nash, 1974.

———. *How to Discipline with Love.* New York: Rawson, 1977

Feingold, Ben. *Why Your Child Is Hyperactive.* New York: Random House, 1975.

Ford, Edward E., and Englund, Steven. *For the Love of Children.* New York: Anchor/Doubleday, 1977.

Forer, Lucille. *The Birth Order Factor.* New York: McKay, 1976.

Gardner, Richard A. *Understanding Children.* New York: Aronson, 1973.

———. *The Parents' Book About Divorce.* New York: Doubleday, 1977.

Gesell, Arnold; Ilg, Frances L.; and Ames, Louise Bates. *The Child from Five to Ten.* New York: Harper & Row, rev. ed., 1974.

Grollman, Earl A. *Explaining Death to Children.* Boston: Beacon Press, 1967.

———. *Explaining Divorce to Children.* Boston: Beacon Press, 1969.

Hautzig, Esther. *Life with Working Parents.* New York: Macmillan, 1977.

Hedges, William D. *At What Age Should Children Enter First Grade: A Comprehensive Review of the Research.* Ann Arbor, Mich.: University Microfilms International, 1977. (300 North Zeeb Road)

Ilg, Frances L.; Ames, Louise Bates; Gillespie, Clyde; and

Haines, Jacqueline. *School Readiness.* New York: Harper & Row, rev. ed., 1978.

Jones, Hettie. *How to Eat Your ABC's: A Book about Vitamins.* New York: Four Winds Press, 1976.

LeShan, Eda. *How to Survive Parenthood.* New York: Random House, 1965.

————. *Learning to Say Goodbye: When A Parent Dies.* New York: Macmillan, 1976.

Levine, Milton, and Seligman, Jean. *The Parents' Encyclopedia of Infancy, Childhood and Adolescence.* New York: Crowell, 1973.

Liepmann, Lise. *Your Child's Sensory World.* New York: Dial, 1973.

McIntire, Roger W. *For Love of Children.* Del Mar, Calif.: CRM Books, 1970.

Maynard, Fredelle. *Guiding Your Child to a More Creative Life.* New York: Doubleday, 1973.

Pantell, Robert H.; Fries, James F.; and Vickery, Donald M. *Taking Care of Your Child: A Parents' Guide to Medical Care.* New York: Addison-Wesley, 1977.

Peck, Ellen. *The Joy of the Only Child.* New York: Delacorte, 1977.

Postman, Neil, and Weingartner, Charles. *The School Book.* New York: Delacorte, 1973.

Schiff, Harriet Sarnoff. *The Bereaved Parent.* New York: Crown, 1977.

Sheldon, William H. *Varieties of Temperament.* New York: Hafner, 1970.

Smith, Lendon. *Improving Your Child's Behavior Chemistry.* Englewood Cliffs, N.J.: Prentice-Hall, 1976.

Thomas, Alexander, and Chess, Stella. *Temperament and Development.* New York: Brunner/Mazel, 1977.

Warner, Silas, and Rosenberg, Edward B. *Your Child Learns Naturally.* New York: Doubleday, 1977.

Wunderlich, Ray. *Allergy, Brains and Children Coping.* St. Petersburg, Fla.: Johnny Reads Press, 1973.

Young, Milton A. *Buttons Are to Push.* New York: Pitman, 1970.

# NOTES

1. From Fredelle Maynard, *Guiding Your Child to a More Creative Life* (New York: Doubleday, 1973), p. 17. This book is highly recommended to any parent interested, as the title indicates, in guiding his or her child to a more creative life.
2. Louise Bates Ames, *Is Your Child in the Wrong Grade?* (New York: Programs for Education, 1978).
3. Frances L. Ilg, Louise Bates Ames, Clyde Gillespie, and Jacqueline Haines, *School Readiness,* rev. ed. (New York: Harper & Row, 1978).
4. John J. Austin, *The First Grade Readiness Checklist* (Muskegon, Mich.: Research Concepts, 1972).
5. Stella Chess, Alexander Thomas, and Herbert G. Birch, *Your Child Is a Person: A Psychological Approach to Parenthood without Guilt* (New York: Viking, 1965).
6. Louise Bates Ames and Frances L. Ilg, *Your Four-Year-Old* (New York: Delacorte, 1976).
7. For an extremely full description of toys and play activities, see Fredelle Maynard, *Guiding Your Child to a More Creative Life* (New York: Doubleday, 1973).

# INDEX

## • *Index* •